TOP **10**
RIO DE JANEIRO

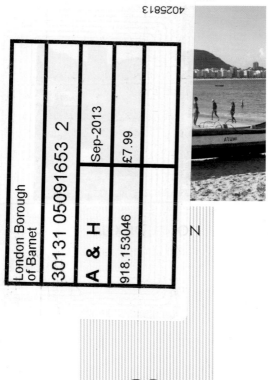

DK
EYEWITNESS TRAVEL

Left **Praia de Copacabana** Right **The statue of Cristo Redentor**

LONDON, NEW YORK,
MELBOURNE, MUNICH AND DELHI
www.dk.com

Design, Editorial and Picture Research, by
Quadrum Solutions, Krishnamai, 33B, Sir
Pochkanwala Road, Worli, Mumbai, India

Printed and bound in China by
Leo Paper Products Ltd

First published in Great Britain in 2009 by Dorling
Kindersley Limited, 80 Strand, London
WC2R 0RL, A Penguin Company

13 14 15 16 10 9 8 7 6 5 4 3 2 1

Reprinted with revisions 2011, 2013

**Copyright 2009, 2013 © Dorling
Kindersley Limited, London**

A CIP catalogue record is available from the
British Library.

ISBN 978 1 4093 7363 6

Within each Top 10 list in this book, no hierarchy
of quality or popularity is implied. All 10 are, in
the editor's opinion, of roughly equal merit.

Floors are referred to throughout in accordance
with North American usage; ie the "first floor" is
at ground level.

MIX
Paper from
responsible sources
FSC
www.fsc.org FSC™ C018179

Contents

Rio de Janeiro's Top 10

Rio de Janeiro's Highlights   6

Corcovado   8

Parque Nacional da Tijuca   10

Sugar Loaf Mountain   12

Mosteiro de São Bento   14

Museu Nacional de
Belas Artes   16

Jardim Botânico   18

Museu Histórico Nacional   20

Praça XV   22

Praia de Copacabana   24

Ipanema and Leblon
Beachlife   26

Moments in History   30

Festivals and Shows   32

Museums and Art
Galleries   34

Beaches   36

Musical Styles   38

Carnaval Parades
and Balls   40

The information in this DK Eyewitness Top 10 Travel Guide is checked regularly.
Every effort has been made to ensure that this book is as up-to-date as possible at the time of
going to press. Some details, however, such as telephone numbers, opening hours, prices,
gallery hanging arrangements and travel information are liable to change. The publishers
cannot accept responsibility for any consequences arising from the use of this book, nor for
any material on third party websites, and cannot guarantee that any website address in this
book will be a suitable source of travel information. We value the views and suggestions of
our readers very highly. Please write to: Publisher, DK Eyewitness Travel Guides,
Dorling Kindersley, 80 Strand, London WC2R 0RL, UK, or email travelguides@dk.com.

Left **Estádio do Maracanã** Center **Portrait of Emperor Dom Pedro I** Right **A** *samba* show

Soccer	42
Restaurants	44
Bars and Nightclubs	46
Activities for Children	48
Sports and Outdoor Activities	50
Tours and Excursions	52
Shopping	54

Around Town

Centro	58
The Guanabara Bay Beach Neighborhoods	66
Lagoa, Gávea, and Jardim Botânico	72
Santa Teresa and Lapa	80
Copacabana, Ipanema, and Leblon	86
Rio de Janeiro State	94

Streetsmart

Planning Your Visit	102
Getting There and Around	103
General Information	104
Banking and Communications	105
Gay and Lesbian Rio	106
Budget Tips	107
Health and Security	108
Things to Avoid	109
Dining Tips	110
Accommodation Tips	111
Places to Stay	112
General Index	118
Phrase Book	126
Street Index	128

Contents

Left **A cable car making its way up the Sugar Loaf** Right **Ceiling of Nossa Senhora de Lapa**

Key to abbreviations: Adm *admission charge* **Av** *Avenida* **Btwn** *between*
Dis. access *disabled access* **s/n** *sem número ("no number" in street address)*

3

RIO DE JANEIRO'S TOP 10

Rio de Janeiro's
Highlights
6–7

Corcovado
8–9

Parque Nacional
da Tijuca
10–11

Sugar Loaf Mountain
12–13

Mosteiro de São Bento
14–15

Museu Nacional
de Belas Artes
16–17

Jardim Botânico
18–19

Museu Histórico
Nacional
20–21

Praça XV
22–23

Praia de Copacabana
24–25

Ipanema and Leblon
Beachlife
26–27

Top Ten of Everything
30–55

RIO DE JANEIRO'S TOP 10

🔟 Rio de Janeiro's Highlights

Rio is so beautiful that the locals, known as "Cariocas," claim that after God spent six days making the world, he rested on Sunday in Rio. Not that they ever call their city Rio – they simply refer to it as "a cidade maravilhosa" or "the wonderful city." And despite its social problems, the city, like its people, is warm, captivating, musical, and devoted to enjoying itself. Rio is a city of neighborhoods, each with its own distinct character, and a different unforgettable view of Corcovado, the mountain that is crowned by a magnificent statue of Christ, who watches over Rio with his arms spread out in perpetual welcome.

Parque Nacional da Tijuca 2

One of the world's largest tracts of urban rain forest, this park has abundant wildlife, waterfalls, and diverse biomes *(see pp10–11)*.

Corcovado 1

The Christ statue atop this mountain was voted one of the seven wonders of the modern world in 2007. Sunset views from here are wonderful *(see pp8–9)*.

Sugar Loaf Mountain 3

This boulder-shaped mountain at the southern end of Botafogo beach boasts magnificent views. The summit is best reached by cable car *(see pp12–13)*.

Mosteiro de São Bento 4

This Baroque church and Benedictine abbey was founded in 1590, although most of its beautiful gilt interior dates from the 17th century *(see pp14–15)*.

Museu Nacional de Belas Artes 5

The country's first art gallery displays Brazilian works from colonial times to the late 20th century, as well as works by international masters such as Debret and Rodin *(see pp16–17)*.

Morro Dona M...

Parque Nacional da Tijuca

Parque Lage

Lagoa

Morro Sau...

Morro Cabrito

RUA PASHAÇO LEÃO
AVENIDA BORGES DE MEDEIROS
RUA JARDIM BOTÂNICO
AV. EPITÁCIO PESSOA
AV. VISCONDE DE ALBUQUERQUE

Jóquei Clube Brasileiro

Lagoa Rodrigo de Freitas

6

Leblon

AVENIDA EPITÁCIO PESSOA

Morro Cantag...

Ipanema

AV. GEN. SAN MARTIN
AV. DELFIM MOREIRA
AVENIDA ATAULFO
RUA VISCONDE DE PIRAJÁ
AVENIDA VIEIRA SOUTO

🔟 Praia do Leblon

🔟 Praia do Ipanema

750 ⊢ yards ⌐ 0 ⌐ meters ⊢ 750

Previous pages **Cristo Redentor overlooking Rio city**

Jardim Botânico
6 Rio's botanical gardens were founded in 1808 by Prince Regent Joāo, and preserve nearly 8,000 species of plants. The orchids are particularly noteworthy *(see pp18–19)*.

Museu Histórico Nacional
7 This museum explores Brazilian history from prehistoric times, with replica rock paintings from the Serra da Capivara, through to the early days of the republic *(see pp20–21)*.

Praça XV
8 This square was the focal point of Rio in colonial times and has one of the city's largest concentrations of pre-20th-century buildings *(see pp22–3)*.

Praia de Copacabana 9
One of the world's most famous urban beaches *(above)* stretches for 2.5 miles (4 km) from the Morro do Leme, at the northern end, to Arpoador in the south. This tourist hub is renowned for its New Year celebrations *(see pp24–5)*.

Ipanema and Leblon Beachlife
10 The Atlantic Ocean laps against the shores of Rio's most desirable beaches, just south of Copacabana. The beaches front fashionable neighborhoods, which are a magnet for tourists *(see pp26–7)*.

TOP 10 Corcovado

The iconic statue of Cristo Redentor (Christ the Redeemer) watches over Rio de Janeiro from atop the 2,316-ft (706-m) high Corcovado, a mountain that derives its name from the Portuguese word corcova (hunchback), which reflects its shape. The winning design in a competition for a grand monument to represent the spirit of Rio de Janeiro, it was inaugurated in 1931 and has, in its short lifetime, come to symbolize Brazil. The journey to Christ's feet – through the charming streets of Cosme Velho neighborhood and the beautiful tropical Parque Nacional da Tijuca (see pp10–11), or up the mountainside on the little funicular – is as rewarding as the panorama from the summit.

Cafés near the statue

⏱ Do not walk back from Corcovado after dark. Muggings are common on the park road and the street lighting is poor.

🥤 Drinks are expensive in the cafés so bring plenty of water.

- Map M1
- Rua Cosme Velho 513, Corcovado
- (021) 2558 1329
- Open 8am–7pm daily
- Funicular railway (Trem do Corcovado): US$22; organized tour: US$8; or taxi; you cannot drive your own vehicle up to Corcovado
- Arrange organized tours through Bel-Tour: (021) 2597 2049
- www.corcovado.com.br

Top 10 Features

1. Cristo Redentor
2. The Chapel at the Base of the Statue
3. Art Deco Features
4. The Forest Setting
5. Refreshments
6. Sunsets and Sunrises
7. Lookout Points
8. Helicopter Tours
9. The Trem do Corcovado
10. The Trem do Corcovado Museum

1 Cristo Redentor
Embracing the city with open arms, the magnificent 98-ft (30-m) tall statue of Jesus Christ *(center)* was designed by Brazilian Heitor da Silva Costa, and draws inspiration from Leonardo Da Vinci's famous study of the human body. The structure was hauled up the mountain in pieces and took years to assemble.

2 The Chapel at the Base of the Statue
Underneath the figure, facing away from the sea, this small chapel is a haven of peace amid the tourist crowds. Mass is held here on Sunday mornings.

3 Art Deco Features
The figure was carved from blocks of soapstone *(left)* by French Art Deco sculptor Paul Landowski, who was also responsible for the monumental Art Deco statue of St. Geneviève in Paris.

4 The Forest Setting
Corcovado is surrounded by the Parque Nacional da Tijuca. The views across the canopy are beautiful in the late afternoon when the setting sun burns a deep orange behind the trees.

5 Refreshments
The bars and restaurants behind and below the statue offer cold drinks, light meals, and welcome shade from the tropical sun.

6 Sunsets and Sunrises
To catch the classic view of Rio *(above)*, come early in the morning or late in the day when the light is soft and the sun is either rising from the bay or setting behind the Floresta da Tijuca *(see p10)*.

7 Lookout Points
There are panoramic views out over the city and Guanabara Bay from the platform at Christ's feet. The platforms behind and below the statue offer fantastic views of Parque Nacional da Tijuca.

8 Helicopter Tours
Flights by helicopter *(above)* offer breathtaking views of the statue and Corcovado *(see p53)*. The early morning provides the best light to enhance the experience.

10 The Trem do Corcovado Museum
This museum *(above)* explores the history of the railway and the Christ statue. On display is the original 19th-century carriage and engine.

9 The Trem do Corcovado
The funicular railway *(below)* runs from Cosme Velho to the summit. Older than the Christ statue, it opened in 1884.

A Seventh Wonder
In 2007 Rio's Cristo Redentor was declared one of the winners in a worldwide poll to find the "New Seven Wonders of the World" – a modern version of Greek historian Herodotus' list from the 5th century BC. Held by the non-profit organization New Open World Corporation, the poll is thought to have been the largest ever, with 100 million voters.

> When the statue was opened in 1931 its lights were switched on from Rome using a signal sent by Marconi, the inventor of radio.

Parque Nacional da Tijuca

This stunning national park contains the lush Floresta da Tijuca (Tijuca Forest), one of the world's largest urban forests, which carpets the hills and coastal mountains that cut through the center of the city. It also features the dramatic Serra de Carioca (Carioca Mountains), the awe-inspiring monolith of Pedra de Gávea, and the Cristo Redentor statue, which looms over the city from the top of Corcovado (see pp8–9). Home to countless species of plants, birds, and mammals, as well as waterfalls and natural springs, this peaceful forest, which covers 15 sq miles (39 sq km), is a little piece of paradise.

Os Esquilos restaurant

🗣 Winding trails, many without signposts, make it easy to lose your way, so it is best to either come on a tour or hire a guide.

🍴 Bring bottled water and a snack. There are very few restaurants in the park.

• Visitors' Center: Map D4; Praça Afonso Viseu, Tijuca; (021) 2492 2253; open 8am–5pm daily
• Os Esquilos: Estrada Barão D'Escragnole, Alto da Boa Vista, Tijuca; (021) 2492 2197
• For tours with Rio Hiking visit www. riohiking.com.br

Top 10 Features

1. Os Esquilos
2. Trails and Walks
3. Cascatinha do Taunay
4. Pedra da Gávea
5. Hang Gliding
6. Wildlife
7. The Mayrink Chapel
8. Park Roads
9. Mirante Dona Marta
10. Mirante Andaime Pequeno

Os Esquilos
A favorite lunch spot on Sundays for wealthy Cariocas, Os Esquilos or "Squirrels" restaurant, is romantically situated under the shade of trees in the heart of this park.

Trails and Walks
A multitude of trails *(right)* cut through Floresta da Tijuca. The lengths of these walks can vary greatly. There are full-day hikes to the park's highest points, at Pedra da Gávea and Pico da Tijuca.

Cascatinha do Taunay
The most accessible of the numerous waterfalls that lie in Floresta da Tijuca can be found just off the road a few miles from the Alto da Boa Vista park gate *(left)*. Its spectacular cascades plummet from a height of 100 ft (30 m).

Pedra da Gávea
Said to be the world's largest coastal monolith, this granite boulder *(above)* on the forest's edge overlooks Rio's suburbs and the Atlantic Ocean.

Hang Gliding 5
A very popular hang-gliding spot *(right)*, the Pedra Bonita (another monolith) is next to Pedra da Gávea and is accessible by road and a short trail. Flights can be fixed through tour operators *(see p50)*.

Wildlife
The endemic wildlife in Parque Nacional da Tijuca includes primates such as the tiny tufted-eared marmoset, as well as 200 species of birds, many of which are endangered.

The Mayrink Chapel
This tiny chapel *(above)* was built in 1863. The panels inside are replicas of paintings by the Brazilian Modernist artist Cândido Portinari. The original works are in the Museu Nacional de Belas Artes *(see pp16–17)*.

Mirante Dona Marta
This lookout, which is perched above the beachfront neighborhood of Botafogo, boasts breathtaking views of the Sugar Loaf *(see pp12–13)*. Note that this area is not safe to visit after dark.

Mirante Andaime Pequeno
This is another fantastic lookout point, which looms over the Jardim Botânico neighborhood. It offers sweeping vistas across emerald-green treetops to the striking Corcovado and Cristo Redentor.

Park Roads
A series of roads *(below)* run through the park, connecting the neighborhoods of Santa Teresa, Jardim Botânico, and Barra da Tijuca. Route maps are available in the visitors' center.

Reforestation in Imperial Rio

Deforestation of Tijuca to make room for sugar and coffee plantations during the early years of colonial rule led to such bad flooding that Emperor Dom Pedro II commissioned its reforestation in 1861. It took 13 years for army major Manuel Gomes Archer and six unnamed African slaves to re-plant the forest with native and exotic trees.

TOP 10 Sugar Loaf Mountain

Rio is a city of magnificent views and none are more breathtaking than those from the top of the 1,312-ft (400-m) high granite and quartz Pão de Açúcar (Sugar Loaf) that sits at the mouth of Guanabara Bay. The mountain's sides are shrouded in remnants of the forest that once covered the whole of Rio de Janeiro and which still provide refuge for marmosets, tanagers, and numerous birds. These are a common sight on the trails that run around the monolith's summit. Come early in the day or right after it has rained for the clearest air and best views from both the Sugar Loaf and its equally impressive monolithic neighbor – Morro da Urca.

Helipad at Morro da Urca

You will need at least three hours to see both the Sugar Loaf and Morro da Urca at a leisurely pace.

There are cafés on both hills and drinks and snacks are available from the the cable-car station in Urca.

- Map J4
- Av Pasteur 520, Urca
- (021) 2546 8400
- Cable cars leave from Urca every 20 minutes
- Open 8am–7:50pm
- Adm US$26

Top 10 Features

1. The Cable Car
2. Morro da Urca
3. Helicopter Tours
4. Bars and Cafés
5. Walks at the Summit
6. Rock Climbing
7. Views of the City
8. The Sugar Loaf
9. Wildlife
10. The Path up Morro da Urca

The Cable Car

The cable car *(below)* runs from the suburb of Urca to the summit of the Sugar Loaf via Morro da Urca, making the hills accessible to people of all levels of fitness. Those looking for a hike can also walk up to the summit.

Helicopter Tours

Flights out over the iconic triumvirate of Sugar Loaf, Corcovado, and the massive Estádio do Maracanã leave from Morra da Urca and Lagoa Rodrigo de Freitas *(see p72)*, which lies just to the north of Ipanema.

Morro da Urca

From Corcovado, the Sugar Loaf resembles a sphinx *(below)*, whose body is made up of Morro da Urca – a separate, lower boulder mountain with a flat summit.

There have been cable cars running up the hills since 1912.

5 Walks at the Summit

Winding trails meander around the summit of the Sugar Loaf. Walks lead through shady forests abundant with tropical birds and butterflies, and lead to a multitude of lookout points.

4 Bars and Cafés
Set in the shade of trees, bars and cafés *(above)* around the Sugar Loaf offer welcome respite from the sun.

6 Rock Climbing
Tour agencies offer rock-climbing trips *(see p51)* suitable for both experienced and novice climbers *(below)*. However, Rio's stunning views make not looking down a challenge.

7 Views of the City
There is a dramatic, 360-degree view out over Rio, Guanabara Bay, and the surrounding rain forest-covered mountains from a variety of lookout points located on both Morro da Urca and Sugar Loaf Mountain.

8 The Sugar Loaf
The Sugar Loaf is one of the highest points above sea level in Rio de Janeiro and is reachable by cable car from Morro da Urca. The first recorded solo climb of the Sugar Loaf was made by British nanny Henrietta Carstairs in 1817.

9 Wildlife
Tufted-eared marmosets *(below)* and various species of rare birds, including the seven-colored tanager, are a common sight on the Sugar Loaf. The trees are adorned with bromeliads and orchids.

10 The Path up Morro da Urca
The Pista Cláudio Coutinho starts from the suburb of Urca, next to Praia Vermelha, and connects to a trail up to the summit of Morro da Urca. Allow at least one hour for the walk and carry plenty of water *(see p69)*.

Pão de Açúcar

The name of Sugar Loaf, adopted in the 19th century, is assumed to have been derived from the rock's shape, which resembles the conical clay molds once used to refine sugar. The indigenous Tupi Guarani people, however, called it "*Pau-nh-acuqua*" (high, pointed, or isolated hill).

Mosteiro de São Bento

The Benedictines, the first religious order to firmly establish itself in Brazil, founded this magnificent hilltop monastery and church in 1590, just to the north of the city center. The church is dedicated to Our Lady of Montserrat, one of the black Madonnas of Europe, and boasts richly decorated interiors that date from the 18th century – the formative years of Brazilian Baroque. The elaborate interior of the church took almost 70 years to complete and was the life work of a series of artists, notably the Benedictine monk Frei Domingos da Conceição (1643–1718).

Gilt ornamentation

🚫 Photography of any kind is not permitted in the church.

🥤 There are no drinks available at the monastery, so be sure to carry water.

- Map W1
- Rua Dom Gerardo 68, Centro (entrance by elevator at No. 40)
- (021) 2206 8100
- Open 7am–5:30pm daily
- www.osb.org.br

Top 10 Features

1. Façade
2. Gilt Ornamentation
3. Baroque Doors
4. Statue of St. Benedict
5. Statue of St. Scholastica
6. Statue of Our Lady of Montserrat
7. The Blessed Sacrament Chapel
8. Paintings by Frei Ricardo Pilar
9. Candelabras
10. The Library

Façade
The unadorned, sober façade of the monastery (center), with its white-washed plaster, raw stone masonry, and squat geometrical towers contrasts starkly with the gilded opulence within.

Gilt Ornamentation
The Brazilian Baroque interior of the church is considered the most ornate in Rio de Janeiro, with almost every square inch richly decorated with gold leaf.

Baroque Doors
The elaborately carved Baroque doors *(left)* that provide access to the nave are considered to be the work of Frei Domingos da Conceição. They are thought to have been carved in the period between 1699 and the monk's death in 1718.

The church underwent several restorations in the 18th, 19th, and 20th centuries.

4 Statue of St. Benedict

Regarded as one of the crowning achievements of Baroque in Rio de Janeiro, this elaborate statue of the founder of the Benedictine order forms a part of the altarpiece, which is located at the back of the church.

5 Statue of St. Scholastica

Another one of Frei Domingos da Conceição's works, this intricately carved statue *(left)* depicts St. Scholastica, who was the twin sister of St. Benedict. The saint's name stands for "she who is devoted to theological study."

6 Statue of Our Lady of Montserrat

This statue of the patron saint of the church was also created by Frei Domingos da Conceição. There are many other paintings of the patron saint adorning the walls of the church and monastery *(right)*.

7 The Blessed Sacrament Chapel

This chapel is the most sacred part of the church. It preserves the consecrated host – bread that Catholics believe to be the body of Christ – and has the most lavish Rococo features of any building in Rio, with gilded carvings and a burnished sacred heart.

8 Paintings by Frei Ricardo Pilar

The painting *Christ of the Martyrs* by the German Benedictine monk Ricardo Pilar dates from 1690 and is the finest of all his paintings in the church.

9 Candelabras

The church was originally illuminated by candles held in ornate candelabras cast from silver by the artist Mestre Valentim. The most impressive of these still sit next to the altarpiece.

The Library 10

The monastery's library *(right)* preserves one of the finest collections of ancient religious books in Brazil. It is open only to those members of the public who have requested permission in writing from the abbot.

St. Benedict

St. Benedict of Norsia, the founder of Western monasticism, was a Roman noble who fled the city to live as a hermit. Inspired by his saintliness, the community of a nearby abbey requested St. Benedict to be their leader. He later founded a monastery, where he wrote the Rule of the Benedictine Order.

Museu Nacional de Belas Artes

Housing the most comprehensive collection of Brazilian art in the country, the National Museum of Fine Arts was established in 1937 in the former Brazilian Academy of Fine Arts building. The architect responsible for the building, Adolfo Morales de Los Rios, was inspired by the Musée du Louvre in Paris, and the building echoes the French-inspired architecture that appears all over Rio de Janeiro. The museum's collection comprises close to 20,000 pieces, including fine, decorative, and popular art. The majority of works are Brazilian and date from the 17th to the 20th centuries. A small part of the collection is foreign and predominantly from Europe.

Tarsila do Amaral's Le Manteau Rouge

🔾 Visit during the week in the middle of the day when Rio is at its hottest and the gallery is less busy.

🔾 The Teatro Municipal, across Avenida Rio Branco in Cinelândia, has an excellent café *(see p63)*.

- Map X4
- Av Rio Branco 199, Centro
- (021) 2219 8474
- Open 10am–6pm Tue–Fri, noon–5pm Sat, Sun & hols
- Adm US$1.50 (free on Sun)
- www.mnba.gov.br

Top 10 Features

1. The Sculpture Gallery
2. Pernambuco Landscapes
3. *Café* by Portinari
4. *Batalha do Avaí*
5. Works by Tarsila do Amaral
6. *Portadora de Perfumes*
7. *Primeira Missa no Brasil*
8. European Engravings
9. Rodin's *Meditação Sem Braço*
10. Almeida's *Arrufos*

1 The Sculpture Gallery

A corridor lined with statues looking out from arcades on to a central space, this gallery *(center)* houses works that include classical reproductions and original pieces by artists such as Rodin and Brecheret.

2 Pernambuco Landscapes

Some of the earliest Brazilian landscapes were painted in the 17th century by expatriate artists in Dutch-occupied Pernambuco. The most famous of these artists was Franz Post.

3 Café by Portinari

Painter Cândido Portinari – a graduate of Rio's Escola Nacional de Belas Artes – is one of Brazil's most influential Modernist painters. His work falls into two periods: *Café (left)* is an example of Social Realism and draws inspiration from Mexican muralists such as Diego Rivera, while most of his other work is Expressionistic.

More Modernist and contemporary paintings can be found in the Museu de Arte Moderna **See p35**.

4 Batalha do Avaí

Pedro Américo's epic work, a majestic mock-European canvas *(above)*, depicts the decisive battle of the 1868 war between Paraguay and the triple alliance of Uruguay, Argentina, and Brazil.

5 Works by Tarsila do Amaral

Do Amaral and her husband, Oswald de Andrade, defined the first distinctly Brazilian approach to art, which they termed *antropofagismo*. This involved adapting western themes to Brazilian contexts.

6 Portadora de Perfumes

Victor Brecheret is Brazil's most highly respected sculptor and was one of the foremost practitioners of Art Deco in Latin America. His work can be seen in many cities in Brazil. *Portadora de Perfumes* was cast from bronze in 1923.

7 Primeira Missa no Brasil

Created in 1861 by Victor Meirelles, this painting *(above)*, fully restored in 2006, depicts the moment the Portuguese first recited mass on Brazilian soil.

8 European Engravings

One of the museum's collections preserves an important archive of engravings and pencil drawings by a number of famous European painters and illustrators including Goya, Doré, and Picasso.

9 Rodin's Meditação Sem Braço

The Modernist sculptor's tortured *Meditação Sem Braço* (Meditation Without Arms) was acquired for the museum by Brazilian billionaire Roberto Marinho.

10 Almeida's Arrufos

Avant-garde painter Belmiro de Almeida traveled to Europe in the 1880s where he absorbed cutting-edge styles. *Arrufos (above)*, painted in 1887, is considered to be his masterpiece.

The French Cultural Mission

When the Portuguese royal family arrived in Rio in 1808, they were determined to turn it into a European-style city. In 1816 they invited the Frenchman Joaquim Le Breton to head a cultural mission to establish European high culture in the city. One of his first endeavors was to establish the Academy of Fine Arts.

Jardim Botânico

Tucked away behind Lagoa Rodrigo de Freitas and Ipanema beach, Rio's shady Jardim Botânico offers a haven of peace from the sweaty urban rush. Founded by Prince Regent João in 1808 as a temporary repository for imported plants to become acclimatized to the tropics, the gardens were reserved for the aristocracy until they opened to the public after the Proclamation of the Republic in 1889. Plants are grouped in distinct areas linked together by gravel paths and interspersed with streams and waterfalls. The gardens have lent their name to the surrounding neighborhood, which has some excellent restaurants, bars, and clubs.

Detail of a fountain

⏱ The best time to see birds and marmosets here is in the early morning during the week, when visitor numbers are low.

🍴 The Café Botânico serves excellent coffee, juices, and light meals.

- Map K2
- Rua Jardim Botânico 1008
- (021) 3874 1808
- Bus 170 from the center, 573 from Glória and Lapa, or 570 from Copacabana and Ipanema
- Open 8am–5pm daily
- Adm US$3
- www.jbrj.gov.br

Top 10 Features

1. Bird-watching
2. Fountains
3. The Avenue of Palms
4. Museu Casa dos Pilões
5. The Orquidarium
6. Giant Amazon Lilies
7. The Arboretum
8. The Jardim dos Beija-Flores
9. Views of Corcovado
10. The Café Botânico

Bird-watching
The gardens offer some of the best urban bird-watching *in Brazil (above)*. Woodnymphs, foliage-gleaners, thrushes, parakeets, woodcreepers, and aplomado falcons are among the easiest to spot.

Fountains
These lush gardens are relatively quiet, except for the soothing tinkle of running water from the elaborate 19th-century fountains that pepper the grounds. This, and the incessant birdsong, offers a welcome break from the city's noisy streets.

The Avenue of Palms
The stately Avenue of Palms *(left)* is located in the center of the gardens close to a magnificent classical fountain. It is lined with 40-ft (13-m) tall imperial palms, which were planted at the time the gardens were established.

The Instituto de Pesquisas Jardim Botânico do Rio de Janeiro (IPJBRJ) is one of the top botanical research institutions in Brazil.

Museu Casa dos Pilões
4 This simple, whitewashed cottage *(above)*, hidden away near the Orquidarium, was once the center for grinding saltpetre, charcoal, and sulphur into gunpowder for the Royal Rio de Janeiro Gunpowder Factory, which dates from 1808 and is also located in the garden.

Views of Corcovado
9 The gardens boast wonderful views of Corcovado *(see pp8–9)*, which is visible in the distance through the trees. The ideal time for taking photographs is in the late afternoon, when visitors start to leave and the light is the best.

The Jardim dos Beija-Flores
8 This beautiful hummingbird garden has been planted with hundreds of brightly colored flowering plants that attract butterflies, such as the Morpho Blue, as well as more than 20 different species of hummingbird.

The Café Botânico
10 Cariocas visit Jardim Botânico not just to enjoy the stunningly diverse plant life, but also to while away the hours over a coffee or light lunch in this attractive open-air café *(left)*, next to the cactus gardens.

The Orquidarium
5 This part of the garden is home to some of the world's most rare orchids, including the famous *Cattleya (below)*. Some 1,000 tropical orchids are cultivated and preserved here.

Giant Amazon Lilies
6 The world's largest waterlilies *(center)*, the *Victoria amazonica* or *Victoria regia* are cultivated on ponds in the gardens. Discovered in the 19th century, the lily was named for the then British Monarch, Queen Victoria.

The Arboretum
7 The garden is home to some 8,000 plant species, including the many native Brazilian trees in the arboretum, which make up a botanical preserve of global importance.

A Botanical Ark

Brazil has more than 21 million hectares of nature preserves which amount to less than 2 percent of the country's territory. According to botanists, this is far too little to ensure the preservation of many vulnerable natural habitats. Botanical gardens play a crucial role in plant conservation, preserving many rare species.

Museu Histórico Nacional

Rio's largest and most interesting museum is devoted to the human history of Brazil dating from as far back as pre-Columbian times through to the 19th century. Exhibits include paintings, sculptures, photographs, maps, and arms, as well as other historical artifacts. Galleries dedicated to the indigenous tribes of Brazil illustrate their way of life. The colonial, imperial, and republican eras are also well represented. Visitors can see a replica of the prehistoric rock paintings from the Serra da Capivara in the northeast of Brazil, claimed to be the oldest record of human presence in South America.

Portrait in the Memória do Estado Imperial

The museum can be visited on the way to or from Praça XV *(see pp22–3).*

Set aside three hours or more to explore the museum fully.

The museum has an excellent café on the ground floor.

- Map Y3
- Praça Marechal Âncora, Centro
- (021) 2550 9224
- Open 10am–5:30pm Tue–Fri, 2–6pm Sat–Sun
- Adm US$4 (free on Sun)
- www.museu historiconacional. com.br

Top 10 Features

1. Royal Carriages
2. Imperial Thrones
3. Constitution of the Nation
4. Pátio dos Canhões
5. Citizenship in Construction
6. Portuguese Around the World
7. Farmácia Teixeira Novaes
8. Statue of Dom Pedro II
9. Temporary Galleries
10. *Combate Naval do Riachuelo*

Royal Carriages

As the only South American country to have had a monarchy, Brazil retains many vestiges of its royal past. The museum houses the carriages of both Emperor Dom Pedro II and Empress Teresa Christina *(below).*

Façade of the museum

Imperial Thrones

The thrones displayed at the museum *(below)* were the seats of state, used for grand occasions by the Portuguese exiled king, João VI, and by the Brazilian Emperors Dom Pedro I and Pedro II.

Constitution of the Nation

These galleries chart Brazil's path to independence: the War of the Triple Alliance, the abolition of slavery and the social uprising leading to the exile of the Portuguese royal family, and the 1889 Proclamation of the Republic.

Pátio dos Canhões
4 This atrium (left) is filled with rusting cannons, many of which date back to the colonial period. Others come from the UK and France.

Citizenship in Construction
5 Focussing on political, civil, and social rights from 1889 to the present, this exhibition displays paintings of leading historical figures and events, as well as videos of 20th-century life in Brazil.

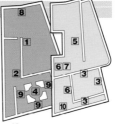

Key
■	1st Floor
■	2nd Floor

Portuguese Around the World
6 This area of the museum covers 400 years of history, from the Portuguese colonization of Brazil, through the gold and diamond booms, to the 1822 Proclamation of Independence.

Farmácia Teixeira Novaes
7 A full-scale, mood-lit reproduction of an 18th-century Rio de Janeiro apothecary shop (above), this exhibit also includes a replica of the back office and laboratory.

Statue of Dom Pedro II
8 This romanticized statue by a Carioca sculptor was first exhibited at the 1867 Paris Exhibition and portrays Emperor Dom Pedro II riding a horse.

Temporary Galleries
9 Some of Rio's most exciting visiting shows are displayed here. Information about the exhibitions can be found on the museum website.

The Building
The museum is housed in a former arsenal and retains a wall from the city's first fort – a reminder of Rio's colonial past. The city center was once as grand as that of Buenos Aires, but the hill, the fort, and much of Portuguese Rio was demolished post independence in order to break away from its colonial history.

Combate Naval do Riachuelo
10 Victor Meirelles' grand and sweeping canvas, in the spirit of the European Romantics, idealizes the Brazilian campaign against Paraguay in the War of the Triple Alliance – the only war that Brazil has fought.

 For more on Rio's history **See pp30–31.**

Praça XV

Praça XV was the first area to develop when the Minas Gerais gold rush in the 18th century transformed Rio from a scruffy port town into a wealthy city. The square became a trading center for imported goods, and trade still takes place here in the ramshackle market next to Rua 1 de Março. The historic heart of Rio, Praça XV witnessed the arrival of Portuguese Prince Regent João when he escaped Napoleon in 1808. It also served as the center of Brazil's political power under the Portuguese. Today, Praça XV is dotted with historical buildings and streets. The restoration of the Paço Imperial in the 1980s has acted as a catalyst in bringing culture back to the city center.

Travessa do Comércio

🟢 Avoid visiting on weekends when the square is empty.

🔵 Visit Travessa do Comércio after 6pm for an alfresco beer.

- Map X2
- Igreja Santa Cruz dos Militares: Rua 1 de Março 36 • Paço Imperial and Exhibition Galleries: Praça XV 48; open 12–6pm Tue–Sun • Palácio Tiradentes: Rua Primeiro de Março s/n; open 10am–5pm Mon–Sat, 12pm–5pm Sun & hols; adm US$2 • Igreja de Nossa Senhora do Carmo da Antiga Sé: Rua 1 de Março; open 8am–4pm Mon–Fri, 10am–2pm Sat & Sun • Igreja da Ordem Terceira de Nossa Senhora do Monte do Carmo: Rua Primeiro de Março s/n; open 8am–4pm Mon–Fri

Top 10 Features

1. Igreja Santa Cruz dos Militares
2. Paço Imperial
3. Exhibition Galleries
4. Estação das Barca
5. Palácio Tiradentes
6. Travessa do Comércio
7. Ferry Dock
8. Igreja de Nossa Senhora do Carmo da Antiga Sé
9. Chafariz do Mestre Valentim
10. Igreja da Ordem Terceira de Nossa Senhora do Monte do Carmo

1 Igreja Santa Cruz dos Militares

This was one of Rio de Janeiro's grandest churches when it was built in the 17th century. After being badly damaged in a fire in 1923, it was skillfully restored and still retains a few original details attributed to the celebrated sculptor, Mestre Valentim, who created all of its carvings.

2 Paço Imperial

This modest colonial building *(below)* was built in 1743 as the seat of government. When the Portuguese royal family arrived in Brazil in 1808, a third floor was added and the building became the Imperial Palace.

3 Exhibition Galleries

Today the Paço Imperial serves as a cultural center, hosting some of Rio's best small exhibitions, many of them devoted to the nation's history and to important figures from Brazil's cultural life.

A visit to Praça XV can be combined with a visit to the Museu Histórico Nacional See pp20–21.

Estação das Barcas
With its prominent clock and faux-Baroque architecture, this boat station was the hub of Brazil's international trade – most of which came through Rio.

Palácio Tiradentes
This 1920s palace is the seat of the Legislative Assembly of the State of Rio de Janeiro. A statue of Tiradentes – the first Brazilian to rebel against the Portuguese – stands in front of the building.

Chafariz do Mestre Valentim
This public drinking fountain *(center)* was designed in 1789 by Mestre Valentim, one of the city's most important Baroque artists. It was intended for use by sailors whose boats were moored on the nearby quays.

Igreja da Ordem Terceira de Nossa Senhora do Monte do Carmo
Situated next to the Old Cathedral, this beautiful 18th-century church boasts an opulent interior covered in gilt carvings *(right)*, many of which are by Mestre Valentim.

Travessa do Comércio
This charming pedestrian street is lined with bars and restaurants. Carmen Miranda (see p41) lived in a house in this alley as a young girl.

Ferry Dock
The Portuguese royal family disembarked just to the west of this spot when they arrived here in 1808. Today, ferries leave from the dock *(above)* for Niterói, across the bay.

Igreja de Nossa Senhora do Carmo da Antiga Sé
Known as the Old Cathedral, this church's modest exterior encloses a beautiful interior with a Rococo nave, ceiling panels, and wall carvings.

Mad Queen Maria

The Faculdade Cândido Mendes at Praça XV 101, formerly a Carmelite Convent, was used to incarcerate Portugal's Queen Maria, whose mood oscillated between religious fervor and depression. Her son, João (later King João VI), ruled in her stead as Regent until her death in 1816.

Share your travel recommendations on **traveldk.com**

23

Praia de Copacabana

One of Rio's most celebrated beaches, Copacabana stretches from the Morro do Leme hill in the northeast to the Arpoador rocks in the southwest. It is a year-round tourist hub, famed for its incredible New Year's Eve celebrations. Until the construction of a tunnel connecting the area with Botafogo in 1892, Copacabana was an unspoilt bay with picturesque dunes. The introduction of trams in the early 20th century made the area fashionable, and by the time the Copacabana Palace was built, the neighborhood had more than 30,000 residents. Today, it is one of the most densely populated areas in the world.

Morro do Leme

The beach is floodlit all night, but it is best avoided after dark as criminals often lurk there.

On Sundays the road closest to the beach is closed to traffic, so this is a particularly good day for cycling and jogging along the beachside track that leads west to Barra da Tijuca. There are bicycle hire stands along the beach.

The beach is lined with numerous little cafés and stalls selling cold, fresh coconut milk straight from the shell.

• Map Q5–R3

Top 10 Features

1. Copacabana and Leme Neighborhoods
2. Fishermen
3. Copacabana Palace
4. Beach Soccer
5. Forte Duque de Caxias
6. New Year's Eve
7. Morro do Leme
8. Forte de Copacabana
9. Beach Vendors
10. Mosaic Pavements

1 Copacabana and Leme Neighborhoods

Copacabana beach fronts two neighborhoods – Leme and Copacabana itself. The area is filled with hotels, vibrant restaurants and bars, and eclectic shops.

2 Fishermen
In the late 19th century, southern Copacabana was home only to a fort and a tiny fishing community, whose descendants own the colorful fishing boats *(left)* that sit on the sand next to Forte de Copacabana.

3 Copacabana Palace
Many famous visitors have stayed at this grand Art Deco hotel *(right)*. Pictures of past celebrity guests are displayed on the second floor *(see p112)*.

Beach Soccer
4 The beach, which is several times wider than a soccer field is long, is the place where *favela* kids have long honed their soccer skills *(above)*.

Forte Duque de Caxias
5 This 18th-century fort, a steep climb from the beach, is named for the general who fought in the 1868 War of the Triple Alliance against Paraguay. Views from here are spectacular.

New Year's Eve
6 Copacabana hosts Rio's biggest New Year's Eve party, when as many as 2 million people gather to listen to concerts and watch the midnight fireworks *(below)*.

Morro do Leme
7 Copacabana is marked by a monolith – the Morro do Leme – which is partially covered with forest. Take the trails up the hill at weekends when guards monitor the entrance.

Forte de Copacabana
8 This fort at the southern end *(above)* affords great views along the beach. A museum here charts the history of the army in Brazil from colonial times.

Beach Vendors
9 Beer, snacks like the *biscoito o globo*, sun umbrellas, *cangas*, flip-flops, and massage are all offered by itinerant beach vendors *(left)*, who walk on the beach from dawn to dusk.

Mosaic Pavements
10 Copacabana's unique black-and-white wave-patterned pavements *(right)* form a beachfront promenade that is typically Portuguese in style. They were designed by Brazilian landscape architect Roberto Burle Marx.

What's in a Name?
Copacabana takes its name from a Bolivian town on the shores of Lake Titicaca, where stood an effigy of Our Lady of Copacabana, believed to bring luck to sailors. The captain of a Spanish galleon thought he was saved from shipwreck by praying to Her, and built a chapel in Her honor near the Arpoador Rocks. This chapel gave the beach its name.

If you visit Copacabana at night, it is safer to take a taxi.

Ipanema and Leblon Beachlife

Urban Rio's most beautiful, fashionable, and secure beaches – Ipanema and its extension farther south, Leblon – offer a wealth of different beachside activities, from sunbathing to keeping in shape. Most tourists make their base at two of Rio's wealthiest neighborhoods located behind the beaches, (also called Ipanema and Leblon), where chic boutiques and glamorous restaurants line the narrow streets. Although the city center is 9 miles (15 km) away, neighboring Copacabana, as well as the Jardim Botânico, Corcovado, and Gávea, are easily accessible from here.

A beachside café

⊘ Avoid walking on the beach after dark.

⊖ Energy drinks can be bought from juice bars throughout Ipanema and Leblon.

• Ipanema: Map M6–N6
• Leblon: Map L6

Top 10 Features

1. Postos
2. Beachwear
3. Cycling and Running Tracks
4. Beach Exercise
5. Cangas
6. Sand Sculptures
7. Beach Massage
8. Beach Volleyball and Footvolley
9. Children's Play Areas
10. Beachside Cafés

Postos

These concrete bunkers on the beach are more than lifeguard stations – social status in Rio is reflected by the location of your towel on the beach. The closer you are to the most fashionable position of all, near Posto Nove (9) in Ipanema, the higher your status.

Beachwear

The essential Ipanema and Leblon beach kit comprises a *tanga* and *canga* (bikini and sarong) and sunglasses for women, and a *sunga* and *havaianas* (speedos and flip-flops) for men. You can buy these items in the shops behind the beach *(see p54)*.

Cycling and Running Tracks

For health-conscious visitors looking for more than sunbathing and lounging on the sand, there are 2-mile (3.5-km) long cycling and running tracks *(left)* along the entire length of Ipanema and Leblon beaches. The tracks tend to be busiest in the mornings and evenings.

There is good surf at Arpoador beach, which is between Ipanema and Copacabana See pp36–7.

Beach Exercise

4 Alongside a multitude of home-grown beach sports, exercising on the sand in these body-conscious neighborhoods is a vanity fair. A popular spot for this is around the pull-up bars *(left)* in front of Rua Farme de Amoedo, which is the posing ground for the most tanned and toned.

Cangas

5 *Cangas* (sarongs) are sold on the beach by wandering vendors. Popular designs include the wave pattern found on the pavements that line the beach, and the Brazilian flag.

Sand Sculptures

6 *Carioca* artists create elaborate fantasy castles and sculptures from Ipanema's fine sand *(above)*. Look out for them right next to the running tracks.

Beach Massage

7 Massages on makeshift couches *(below)* and chairs have been available on Ipanema and Leblon for decades, and tend to be of a very high standard.

Children's Play Areas

9 For a family outing, there are children's play areas *(below)* at the Baixo Bebê kiosk *(see p48)* on Leblon beach and in Praça Nossa Senhora da Paz, behind Ipanema beach.

Beach Volleyball and Footvolley

8 Brazilians are the best in the world at beach volleyball and the national women's team practice on Ipanema. Footvolley is a variation played entirely with the feet and head *(see p43)*.

Beachside Cafés

10 The beachside cafés that line Ipanema and Leblon beaches serve snacks, drinks, and delicious ice-cold coconut milk, drunk straight from the coconut shell. The cafés also offer shade from the tropical sun.

The Girl from Ipanema

Poet Vinícius de Moraes and composer Antônio Carlos Jobim wrote *The Girl from Ipanema* in homage to a beautiful teenager called Heloisa Pinheiro who, on her way to the beach, used to pass the café where the men would meet for an afternoon beer.

Behind the Os Dois Irmãos peaks at the end of Leblon are two of Rio's largest favelas, Rocinha (see pp74–5) and Vidigal.

Painting depicting Pedro I declaring independence

Moments in History

1 The First Brazilians
Brazil's first inhabitants are believed to have traveled across temporary land bridges connecting Asia and America at the Bering Straits, and then south through the Americas between 40,000 and 12,000 years ago.

2 Portuguese Land in Rio
On January 1, 1502, the Portuguese explorer Gaspar de Lemos arrived in Guanabara Bay, where he built a small fort to claim the bay for Portugal. But hostile confrontations with the indigenous Tamoio people led the Portuguese to establish their colony elsewhere in Brazil.

3 The French Arrive
In 1555, France sent a fleet of ships to Rio, where they claimed a tiny island in Guanabara

Portrait of Emperor Dom Pedro II

Bay. The French treated the Tamoio far better than the Portuguese had done and succeeded in forging a military alliance with them.

4 The Portuguese Defeat the French-Tamoio Alliance
The Portuguese returned to Rio and, with various indigenous groups, fought numerous battles against the French-Tamoio Alliance, eventually defeating it on January 20, 1567.

5 The Portuguese Royal Court Moves to Rio
In November 1807, the entire Portuguese royal family fled Napoleon. Their fleet comprised some 40 ships packed with 15,000 members of the Portuguese court and government. They arrived in Brazil in 1808.

6 The French Cultural Mission
In 1816, King Dom João VI of Portugal invited the French to introduce European culture to Rio by bringing in their styles of architecture, art, and music (see p17).

7 Pedro I Declares Independence
King Dom João VI returned to Portugal in 1821, leaving his son Pedro as Prince Regent in Brazil. Pedro declared independence from Portugal the next year, and crowned himself Emperor Dom Pedro I. He and his son, Pedro II, ruled for the next 67 years.

 Previous pages **Museu de Arte Contemporanea de Niterói**

President Kubitschek on the cover of Time

Top 10 Historical Figures

1 Chief Cunhambebe
The ferocious giant chief of the Tamoio, who almost defeated the Portuguese.

2 Gaspar de Lemos
The first European to see Rio was also present when Alvarez Cabral "discovered" Brazil in 1500.

3 Nicholas de Villegagnon
The Frenchman responsible for claiming an island in Guanabara Bay and forging alliances with the Tamoio.

4 Mem de Sá
One of Portugal's most ruthless and effective generals, Mem de Sá founded Rio along with his 17-year-old nephew, Estácio, in 1565.

5 João VI of Portugal
This Regent fled Portugal in 1808, founded imperial Brazil, and later became King João VI.

6 Emperor Dom Pedro I
Son of João VI, declarer of independence, and the first Emperor of free Brazil.

7 Emperor Dom Pedro II
Pedro I's son, who helped abolish slavery and oversaw the start of industrialization.

8 Marechal Deodoro da Fonseca
The soldier who overthrew Pedro II declared Brazil a republic in 1889 and became its first president.

9 Getúlio Vargas
President from 1930 to 1945 and again from 1951 to his suicide in 1954. He copied the fascist politics of Europe.

10 Juscelino Kubitschek
Promising 50 years of progress in five, this president oversaw economic growth but finally bankrupted Brazil.

8 Brazil Becomes a Republic

The republican movement of 1870 was provoked by general discontent over high taxes and the movement toward the abolition of slavery. On November 15, 1889, Emperor Dom Pedro II was overthrown and the republic was proclaimed by Marechal Deodoro da Fonseca.

9 The Capital Moves from Rio to Brasilia

Rio de Janeiro was the capital of Brazil until 1960, when it was replaced by Brasilia. This change was overseen by President Juscelino Kubitschek and three Modernist architects, Lúcio Costa, Oscar Niemeyer *(see p68)*, and Roberto Burle Marx.

10 Rio Hosts the World Environmental Summit

On June 3, 1992, Rio hosted the Earth Summit – the first and largest global conference of its kind on the environment. It provided an impetus for Brazil to review its own environmental record, leading to great change in the way that the national economy was run.

 Gaspar de Lemos mistook Guanabara Bay for the mouth of a river and named the city the January River – Rio de Janeiro.

Left **New Year's Eve fireworks** Center **Presente de Yemanjá** Right **Cidade Negra performing**

🔟 Festivals and Shows

1 New Year's Eve
Rio's biggest celebration is not Carnaval but Reveillon, or New Year's Eve. Millions gather on Copacabana beach for free concerts and spectacular fireworks displays *(see p25)*. ◈ *Dec 31*

2 Carnaval
Carnaval takes place at the start of Lent in February or March. The parades take place in the Sambódromo stadium.
◈ *Map T4 • Sambódromo, Rua Marquês de Sapucaí, Centro • (021) 2546 8080 • Feb/Mar • Adm*

3 The Festa de Nossa Senhora da Penha
Catholic pilgrims crawl or walk on their knees up the steps to this church for the city's most traditional festival. ◈ *Map D3 • Largo da Penha 19, Penha • (021) 3219 6262 • Oct • www.santuariopenhario.org.br*

4 Festa Literária Internacional de Paraty
This gathering of acclaimed international writers takes place in the pretty little colonial port town of Paraty, which is located three hours south of Rio de Janeiro. There is always plenty of live music and other events on offer here. Past guests have included well-known novelists such as Toni Morrison, Salman Rushdie, and Michael Ondaatje.
◈ *Jul/Aug • www.flip.org.br*

5 Presente de Yemanjá
This New Year's Eve celebration is dedicated to Yemanjá the Orixá, the Goddess of the Sea. Devotees dressed in white gather on beaches around the city from midnight until dawn to worship her and toss offerings in the Atlantic.
◈ *Dec 31*

Colorful Carnaval

6 Festa de São Sebastião

The patron saint of Rio is honored with a series of processions that leave from the church of São Sebastião dos Capuchinos in Tijuca and make their way to the city center. Afro-Brazilian celebrations are also held at Santa Teresa. ✆ *Jan 20*

7 Festas Juninas

These extensive religious festivals are held throughout June in homage to St. Anthony and St. John. Locals dress up in checked shirts, drink spicy wine, feast on traditional food, and dance to lively *forró* music from northeastern Brazilian. ✆ *Jun*

8 Festival Internacional de Cinema do Rio

One of South America's largest and most diverse film festivals, this event showcases independent films from all over the world, with a special focus on Latin America. Full features and shorts are shown in cinemas throughout the city. ✆ *Sep–Oct* • *www.festivaldorio.com.br*

9 Anima Mundi – Festival Internacional de Cinema de Animação

One of the world's premier celebrations of animation show-cases work from mainstream, independent, and avant-garde film-makers the world over. Every year, after it takes place in Rio, it moves on to São Paulo. ✆ *Jul* • *www.animamundi.com.br*

10 Dia do Indio

This celebration commemo-rates the first Inter-American Indigenous Congress, which took place in Mexico City in 1940. Indigenous people from all over Brazil participate. ✆ *Apr 19*

Top 10 Live Acts in Rio

1 Jorge Ben
The founding father of the funky Rio sound plays live every New Year's Eve.

2 Roberto Carlos
Year-end festivities in Rio would not be complete without a show by Latin America's most successful recording artist.

3 Orquestra Imperial
Made up of popular local musicians, this dance-hall *samba*, or *gafieira* band, is a Carnaval party stalwart.

4 Chico Buarque
The political conscience of his generation, Buarque often plays in Ipanema and Lapa.

5 Cidade Negra
Brazil's top reggae band regularly plays to huge audiences over New Year and during Carnaval.

6 Sandra de Sá
The queen of Rio *samba* soul is famous for her covers of classic Motown tracks and is another festival regular.

7 Martinho da Vila
Writer of many of the official Carnaval parade *sambas* for the Unidos de Vila Isabel *samba* school.

8 Zeca Pagodinho
The king of Rio party music plays an infectious variant of *samba* called *pagode (see p38)*.

9 Seu Jorge
One of Brazil's biggest music and movie stars who made his name at the Circo Voador *(see p83)* club in Lapa.

10 Marisa Monte
A trained classical musician, Monte has become one of Rio de Janeiro's biggest international stars.

Left **Museu de Arte Contemporanea de Niterói** Right **Museu Internacional de Arte Naïf**

Museums and Art Galleries

1 Museu Nacional de Belas Artes

This museum holds the largest collection of Brazilian art in the country, dating from colonial times through to the 20th century. International pieces are also on display here *(see pp16–17)*.

2 Museu Histórico Nacional

Housed in a colonial building that served as an arsenal till the 1920s, this fascinating museum features displays charting Brazilian history *(see pp20–21)*.

Imperial seat in Museu Histórico Nacional

3 Museu da República

This Baroque palace, now a museum, was the site of the suicide of Brazil's most influential

A sculpture at Museu Nacional de Belas Artes

statesman. President Vargas *(see p31)* killed himself in his bedroom here in 1954. Exhibits include his nightshirt, with the bullet hole in the breast.

🔊 *Map H3 • Palácio do Catete, Rua do Catete 153 • (021) 3235 2650 • Open 10am–5pm Tue–Fri, 2–6pm Sat, Sun & hols • Adm (free on Wed & Sun)*

4 Museu de Arte Contemporanea de Niterói (MAC)

Contemporary Brazilian art is on display in this museum, which is housed in an iconic building designed by Oscar Niemeyer *(see p68)*. The concrete spheroid sits at the end of a rocky promontory that juts into Guanabara Bay, and the interior is accessed via a long red ramp. 🔊 *Map C5 • Mirante da Boa Viagem s/n, Boa Viagem, Niterói • (021) 2620 2400 • Open 10am–6pm Tue–Sun • Adm • www.macniteroi.com.br*

5 Museu Internacional de Arte Naïf (MIAN)

This delightful museum features one the world's largest collections of Naive art. Some of the Brazilian pieces are by *favela* and rural artists and offer powerful insights into their daily lives. There is also an interesting shop in the museum. 🔊 *Map G3 • Rua Cosme Velho 561, Cosme Velho • (021) 2205 8612 • Open 10am–6pm Tue–Fri, noon–6pm Sat • Adm • www.museunaif.com.br*

6 Museu de Arte Moderna (MAM)

Housed in a modernist building on V-shaped stilts, this museum features works by local artists such as Tarsila do Amaral and Cândido Portinari *(see pp16–17)*, as well as international artists. ⊗ *Map X4 • Av Infante Dom Henrique 85, Parque do Flamengo • (021) 2240 4944 • Open noon–6pm Tue–Fri, noon–7pm Sat, Sun & hols • Adm*
• www.mamrio.com.br

The exterior of Museu de Arte Moderna

7 Estádio do Maracanã

The pavement outside the world's largest soccer stadium is covered in footprints made by star players including Pele. There is a gallery dedicated to soccer greats inside the stadium. ⊗ *Map E2 • Rua Prof Eurico Rabelo • (021) 8871 3950 • Open 9am–1pm daily*

8 Sambódromo and Museu do Carnaval

This stadium, designed by Oscar Niemeyer *(see p68)* and built on the street thought to be the birthplace of *samba*, hosts Carnaval parades. Carnaval relics are displayed in the museum. ⊗ *Map I4 • Rua Marquês de Sapucaí, Praça Onze, Centro • Open 11am–5pm Tue–Sun*

9 Museu Nacional

This crumbling former palace, set in expansive gardens, preserves a diverse collection of items, including the largest meteorite to fall in Brazil, dinosaur bones, and mummies. ⊗ *Map E1 • Quinta da Boa Vista s/n, São Cristóvão • (021) 2562 6900 • Open 10am–4pm Tue–Sun • Adm • www.museunacional.ufrj.br*

10 Ilha Fiscal

This Neo-Gothic folly was once a 19th-century royal pleasure palace that hosted masked balls that later evolved into Carnaval. ⊗ *Map J1 • Av Alfredo Agache, Centro • (021) 2233 9165 • Tours: 12:30pm, 2pm, and 3:30pm Thu–Sun • Adm*

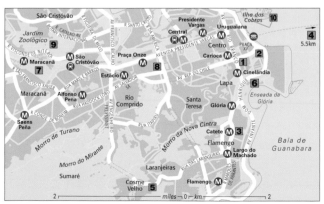

Guided visits to Ilha Fiscal are coordinated by the Espaço Cultural da Marinha **See p48**.

Left **Sunset view from Charitas beach** Right **View of the Sugar Loaf from Flamengo beach**

🔟 Beaches

1 Ipanema and Leblon

These two contiguous neighborhoods have the cleanest, safest, and most beautiful beaches in the city, and are the favorite playgrounds of Rio de Janeiro's upper-middle class *(see pp26–7)*.

2 Copacabana

From the 1930s to the 1970s this fine, broad beach was the trendy place to lay a towel in the city. Since the 1980s, it has grown a little tawdry, especially at night. Sunbathing is best in front of the Copacabana Palace hotel *(see pp24–5)*.

3 Charitas

Cariocas are fond of saying that the best thing about Niterói – the city across Guanabara Bay – is its views of Rio. None are better than those from Charitas beach in the afternoon, when Corcovado and the Sugar Loaf are silhouetted against the setting sun. ◈ *Map C5*

4 Grumari

Surfers head to this beach at Rio's southern end beyond Barra da Tijuca. The clean waters here are also the coolest in the city. There is a powerful undertow, however, which makes it unsuitable for swimming. ◈ *Map A6*

5 São Conrado

This beach, which is a landing point for hang gliders, is popular with local television celebrities, many of whom have expensive apartments in the fortified tower blocks that are sandwiched between the sea and the city's largest *favela*, Rocinha *(see p74)*. ◈ *Map B6*

6 Barra da Tijuca

Rio's largest beach is 11 miles (18 km) long and has both crowded and isolated stretches. It is a favorite with surfers, wind-surfers, and fishing enthusiasts. The suburb is characterized by long avenues, apartment blocks, and shopping malls. ◈ *Map B6*

A surfer at Grumari beach

A fresh drink at a juice bar is a pre-beach ritual in Rio.

A surfing enthusiast at Arpoador beach

Arpoador

7 This beach around the rocky headland at the southern end of Copacabana features cafés, coconut stalls, and juice bars where Cariocas hang out. Strong waves make it popular with surfers but the rocks are unsafe after dark. ◈ *Map P6*

Recreio dos Bandeirantes

8 Despite being very built up, Recreio dos Bandeirantes is a peaceful suburb. The long, straight beach here is pounded by powerful waves, making it a good surf spot. ◈ *Map A6*

Botafogo

9 The Sugar Loaf *(see pp12–13)* sits at the southern end of this perfectly rounded cove, which lies between Copacabana and Centro, at the mouth of the bay. It was a popular bathing spot until the 1960s, when pollution made swimming inadvisable. ◈ *Map S1*

Flamengo

10 This stretch of pearl-white sand is the prettiest of all the Guanabara Bay beaches and affords wonderful views of the bay and the Sugar Loaf. The water is now far too dirty for swimming and the beach itself is unsafe after dark. ◈ *Map Y6*

Top 10 Brazilian Juices

1 Açaí
This purple Amazonian palm berry drink has been popular with locals for thousands of years and is packed with vitamins.

2 Cupuaçu
This pod-like fruit is related to cocoa and has a sweet and pungent juice. The taste is unusual but can be strangely addictive.

3 Camu-Camu
This Amazonian fruit grows by seasonally flooded rivers and has a very high vitamin C content.

4 Taperebá
A refreshing Amazonian fruit juice high in vitamin C. It is also supposed to have antibiotic properties.

5 Acerola
Also known as West Indian cherry juice, this is a refreshing thirst-quencher.

6 Graviola
A sweet white juice made from a relative of the custard apple and *caju*.

7 Caju
The juice of the Amazonian cashew-nut fruit, which is also famous the world over for its nuts.

8 Jabuticaba
A tart, berry-like fruit juice popular in the state of Minas Gerais. The fruit grows directly on tree trunks.

9 Umbu
A sweet fruit juice that comes from a pulpy berry. It is particularly popular in the state of Bahia.

10 Seriguela
This refreshing juice comes from Brazil's woodland savannah, the *cerrado*.

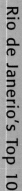

Left **Crowds dancing to baile funk** Right **Musicians performing** *bossa nova*

🔟 Musical Styles

1 Samba
Born in the state of Bahia, *samba* developed in poverty-ridden Rio during the early 20th century. Energetic and passionate, it has influenced nearly every Brazilian musical style and is ubiquitous during Carnaval.

2 Bossa Nova
In the 1950s, an eclectic group of writers, artists, and musicians from Ipanema and Copacabana slowed *samba* down. They added complex harmonies and a lilting guitar style to produce *bossa nova*, best known by Antonio Carlos Jobim's *The Girl From Ipanema*.

3 Choro
This was one of the first musical styles to evolve in the city and is performed by four jazz musicians. The most famous *choro* star and composer of the past is Pixinguinha.

4 Pagode
Pagode evolved at community barbecues in 1970s suburban Rio. It is an infectious, swinging *samba* usually with cheeky macho lyrics, which are sometimes laced with wry social commentary.

5 Gafieira
Born in the grand dance halls of 1950s Rio, when couples put on their weekend best to twist and turn to big *samba* bands, *gafieira* is usually played by an orchestra and accompanied by elegant dancing. It has undergone a renaissance since the early 1990s, especially in Lapa.

6 Suinge and Samba Funk
In the 1970s, *samba* and jazz-funk were fused to produce Rio's most popular dance music – *suinge*. This was sped up in the 1980s into *samba* funk. Both make for excellent live acts.

Performers in a *samba* show

Samba, choro, *and* bossa nova *were all born in Rio.*

Dancing to *gafieira*

Samba Soul
This mix of Brazilian rhythms with American soul singing was created almost single-handedly by Tim Maia – a Carioca who moved to the USA and fell in love with Motown.

Rap Brasileiro
In the 1980s, hip hop music struck a chord with *favela* dwellers. These sounds were fused with *repente* – a rhythmical form of street poetry that dates back to colonial times – and Brazilian percussion to form one of Rio's edgiest sounds.

Baile Funk
A distorted, bass-driven, DJ-spun electronica with rap-vocals and a *pagode* chorus often accompanied by raunchy dancing. Unlike rap, it has little social conscience and focuses on having a good time.

Vanguarda
Brazil has produced some of the world's most distinguished jazz, experimental, and avant-garde musicians. Their erudite, eclectic styles – known collectively as *vanguarda* – are strongly influenced by African and indigenous Brazilian music.

Top 10 Brazilian Musical Instruments

Cavaquinho
This tiny four-stringed Portuguese guitar provides the melodic accompaniment to *samba*. It is related to the ukulele in Hawai'i.

Surdo
The enormous drum that provides the pulsating beat of *samba*.

Repenique
These are hand-held sharp percussion drums, played in unison to create the distinctive rat-a-tat of *samba*.

Tamborim
A very tense, high timbre compact drum used in *pagode* and *choro*. Unlike the tambourine, it has no bells.

Pandeiro
A small, tight drum with side-bells or *platinelas*, the *pandeiro* is used in most Brazilian music.

Timbal
A conical drum of varying sizes that makes up part of a *samba* drum troupe.

Cuica
A friction drum played with cloth, hands, and a wooden stick with a unique crying sound.

Caxixi
A hand-held wicker basket filled with seeds used in the martial art dance *capoeira*.

Berimbau
A long-bowed instrument with a single metal wire that provides the percussive twang in *capoeira*.

Atabaque
A long, conical drum used in *candomblé* (a mix of Catholic and African beliefs) rituals. It can also be a rhythmic accompaniment to *capoeira*.

Left **Banda de Ipanema** Right **Bloco Santa Teresa**

Carnaval Parades and Balls

Sunday and Monday at the Sambódromo

On the first Sunday and Monday of Carnaval, the top *samba* schools march through the Sambódromo *(see p35)* in *blocos* (parades) to compete for the title of champion. The show continues until after dawn. ◈ *Map T4* • *Centro* • *Adm*

Banda de Ipanema

This is one of Carnaval's largest and most colorful street parades. Outrageously dressed transvestite and transsexual partygoers dance *samba* with tourists, revelers, families, and passersby *(see p106)*.

Baile do Copa

Another Carnaval tradition is the formal "Russian Imperial" black-tie ball, which is held at the Copacabana Palace hotel *(see p112)* on the first Saturday of Carnaval. Book tickets through the hotel in advance. ◈ *Map R3* • *Copacabana* • *Adm*

Bloco Santa Teresa

The highlights of this lively street party are its atmosphere and music. It takes place between Largo dos Guimarães and Largo das Neves in Santa Teresa, and is popular with a young crowd. ◈ *Map U5* • *Santa Teresa* • *(021) 2620 2481* • *Adm*

Champions' Parade

The winners of the spectacular Sambódromo parades dance again on the final Saturday of Carnaval. It is easier to get tickets for this event than the earlier performances. ◈ *Map T4* • *Centro* • *(021) 4042 0213* • *Adm*

Bloco Cacique de Ramos

The Bloco Cacique de Ramos parade has marched along Avenida Rio Branco since 1961. A new *samba* song is written and sung every year by one of Rio's famed *sambistas*. ◈ *Map W1–W3* • *Centro* • *(021) 3880 9248* • *Adm*

Bloco de Segunda

Held on the first Monday of Carnaval week, this *bloco* features dancers in elaborate costume, including *Baianas* (Afro-Brazilian women) in enormous flowing dresses who spin as they *samba*. ◈ *Map Q1* • *Botafogo*

Parade at the Sambódromo

The Sambódromo was designed by Oscar Niemeyer (see p68) and opened in 1984.

Colorful reveler at Banda de Ipanema

Banda de Carmen Miranda

8 This *bloco* was created in 1989 in reverence to Carmen Miranda, a Portuguese singer who settled in Brazil and had a penchant for fruit-covered hats. It showcases Brazil's most lavishly costumed drag queens, all of whom faithfully pay homage to their idol. 🕾 *Map M6* • *Ipanema*

Baile Vermelho e Preto do Flamengo

9 *Vermelho* (red) and *preto* (black) are the colors of one of Rio's most popular soccer teams, Flamengo *(see p42)*, and are a compulsory part of the dress code at their annual ball held at the Clube Monte Libano in Lagoa. Costumes are notoriously skimpy and the *sambas* recount past football glories. 🕾 *Map Q1* • *Botafogo* • *(021) 2512 8833* • *Adm*

Gala Gay

10 One of Rio's most famous and lavish indoor Carnaval balls takes place at a different location each year on Carnival Tuesday. The star-studded event is heavily televised and tickets are incredibly hard to secure (see p106).

Top 10 Samba Schools

1 Portela
This school has won the Sambódromo *samba* contest 21 times under a blue and white flag. 🕾 www.sambacity. info/portela.html

2 Mangueira
The popular Mangueira school has won 17 times. Its colors are pink and green. 🕾 www.mangueira.com br

3 Império Serrano
Parading under a green flag, Serrano has had nine victories.

4 Unidos da Tijuca
Winner of multiple gold standards, Tijuca's colors are yellow and blue. 🕾 www. unidosdatijuca.com.br

5 Unidos do Viradouro
The famous Carnaval queen Juliana Paes danced for this school. Orange and white are its colors.

6 Salgueiro
A top school with eight victories, colored red and white. 🕾 www.salgueiro.com.br

7 Estácio de Sá
One-time victors in 2005, its colors are red and white. 🕾 www.gresestaciodesa.com.br

8 Imperatriz Leopoldinense
A successful school with eight victories, its colors are green and white. 🕾 www. imperatrizleopoldinense.com.br

9 Beija Flor de Nilópolis
Flying a blue and white flag, this is the most successful school since 2000, with 10 wins. 🕾 www.beija-flor.com.br

10 Vila Isabel
With two victories to date, this club flies the peach and white flag. 🕾 www. gresunidosdevilaisabel.com.br

Left **Aerial view of Estádio do Maracanã** Right **Rio de Janeiro State Championship match**

Soccer

1 Estádio do Maracanã
The world's largest soccer stadium currently has a seating capacity of 83,000 and is where Pelé scored his 1,000th goal in 1969. The atmosphere at the stadium during a game is electric *(see p35)*.

2 Flamengo
This is one of Rio's four big soccer clubs. Its moment of glory was winning the inaugural Brazilian World Championship in 1981. Famous past players include Gérson, Sócrates, and Zico.

3 Botafogo
This club's ex-players make up a roster of some of the greatest names in Brazilian soccer. Its golden era was in the 1950s and 60s when it provided most of the players for Brazil's victorious World Cup team.

4 Fluminense
Soccer was introduced to Rio de Janeiro by Englishman Oscar Cox, who went on to found Fluminense on July 21, 1902. The club remains one of Rio's most traditional, and many of its supporters are wealthy Cariocas. Its archrival is Flamengo.

Fluminense's insignia

5 Vasco
Named for the Portuguese explorer Vasco da Gama, this club is traditionally supported by Portuguese Cariocas.

6 The Rio-vs-São Paulo Derby
The annual *Torneiro Rio–São Paulo* is a tournament played between teams from the rival states Rio de Janeiro and São Paulo, and is now one of the most bitterly contested events in South American soccer.

Crowds at Maracanã

It is possible to organize seeing a match through a tour company. Visit www.bealocal.com for more information.

Beach soccer

Top 10 Famous Carioca Soccer Stars

1 Leônidas da Silva (1913–2004)
Before Leônidas da Silva, Brazilian soccer was a white, middle-class game.

2 Nilton Santos (b. 1927)
A key defender in three World Cups and scorer of one of the most spectacular goals of all time in a match against Austria in 1958.

3 Carlos Alberto (b. 1944)
Captain of Brazil's World Cup winning team in 1970 and a great defender.

4 Garrincha (1933–83)
Pele's contemporary and officially the best Brazilian player other than Pele himself, according to FIFA.

5 Didi (1929–2001)
A legendary midfielder named player of the tournament at the 1958 World Cup in Sweden.

6 Gérson (b. 1941)
One of the best passers in the history of football, who masterminded the 1970 World Cup victory.

7 Zico (b. 1953)
One of the greatest midfielders in the history of the beautiful game.

8 Jairzinho (b. 1944)
A lightning-fast winger who devastated opponents in the 1970 World Cup.

9 Romário (b. 1966)
The only player other than Pelé to score 1,000 goals in professional soccer.

10 Ronaldo (b. 1976)
Nicknamed "The Phenomenon" in Brazil, he won three FIFA Player of the Year awards.

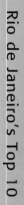

7 The Rio de Janeiro State Championship
The *Campeonato Carioca* was established in 1906. Fluminense and Flamengo, with 30 titles each, have more victories than any other club.

8 The "Maracanazo Tragedy"
"O Maracanazo" refers to the Brazilian soccer "tragedy" during the 1950 World Cup, when Brazil lost to Uruguay. The word has passed into common parlance in Brazil and is used to refer to other soccer defeats and even political debacles.

9 Beach Soccer
Many of Rio's greatest stars learned to play soccer on makeshift pitches on the city's beaches. The players preserved such a love of beach soccer that it is now a FIFA-recognized sport in its own right. ✒ *www.fifa.com*

10 Footvolley
This sport, known as *futevôlei* in Portuguese, began on the beaches of Rio. Its rules are similar to volleyball, but only the feet and head can be used. Brazil remains the leading footvolley team, but is hotly pursued by some Asian nations.

Left **The long, open grill at Zuka** Right **Espírito Santa**

🔟 Restaurants

1 Zuka
Decked out in dark wood and fronted by an open grill, this dining room was set up by a former chef of New York's acclaimed restaurant Nobu. It is now run by one of Rio's most celebrated chefs, Ludmilla Soeiro. Zuka's fusion menu comprises grills, seafood, and excellent salads. ⊗ Map K5 • Rua Dias Ferreira 233, Leblon • (021) 3205 7154 • www. zuka.com.br • $$$$$

2 Roberta Sudbrack
This eponymous restaurant established Roberta Sudbrack as arguably the best chef in South America. The menu features startlingly original dishes that blend *haute cuisine* and molecular gastronomy.
⊗ Map M2 • Rua Lineu de Paula Machado 916, Jardim Botânico • (021) 3874 0139 • www.robertasudbrack.com.br • $$$$$

A dish at Manekineko

3 Olympe
Claude Troisgros – one of the inventors of *nouvelle cuisine* in France – founded this intimate dining room on a quiet street near Lagoa Rodrigo de Freitas. The classic French fare makes use of tropical ingredients.
⊗ Map N2 • Rua Custódio Serrão 62, Lagoa • (021) 2539 4542 • www.claudetroisgros. com.br • $$$$$

4 Antiquarius
One of the city's longest established Portuguese restaurants, Antiquarius oozes old-fashioned style. Celebrities flock here for the famous *bacalhau* (salt-cod) and excellent seafood. The ambience is warm and friendly, though the high prices make this a treat for a special occasion.
⊗ Map K6 • Rua Aristides Espínola 19, Leblon • (021) 2294 1049 • $$$$$

Tables laid out at Fasano

5 Satyricon
Satyricon's smart dining room is dominated by a vast counter covered with myriad varieties of tropical fish, crustaceans, and shellfish on ice. The seafood here is said to be the best in the city and the celebrity clientele includes Ronaldo *(see p99)*.

For more restaurants **See pp63, 71, 77, 85, 91, and 99.**

6 Gero
Set up by celebrated restaurateur Rogério Fasano, this chic, minimalist eatery serves innovative, highly feted Italian food and has a long bar that dominates the dining room. Its sophisticated clientele come here not only for the dining experience, but also to be seen. ⊛ Map M5 • Rua Aníbal de Mendonça 157, Ipanema • (021) 2239 8158 • $$$$$

7 Fasano
Rogério Fasano's sophisticated establishment is one of Rio de Janeiro's finest restaurants and is located in one of its most exclusive hotels. Fasano specializes in fresh seafood and offers exceptionally beautiful views over the Atlantic (see p112).

8 Manekineko
Brazil has more ethnic Japanese than any country in the world outside Japan, and Rio de Janeiro is replete with fine Japanese restaurants. Part of a chain, this restaurant contrasts with the more traditional Sushi Leblon (see p91) a few doors away. Brazilian-Japanese fusion cooking is served here to a lively crowd. The menu changes every few months. ⊛ Map K5 • Rua Dias Ferreira 410, Leblon • (021) 2540 7461 • $$$$

9 Espírito Santa
Santa Teresa is full of funky little restaurants and bars and this is one of the best. Amazonian and Bahian cooking – including exquisite river fish like pacu – is served in an informal

Fresh fish at Satyricon

restaurant-bar and on a small, candle-lit roof terrace, which boasts wonderful views of the city at night. The bartender serves some of Rio's best caipirinhas and the club downstairs opens for dancing on Fridays (see p84).

10 Esplanada Grill
Brazil is famous for its grilled meat restaurants, or churrascarias, and none is better than the Esplanada Grill. It is a popular place for business men and women who appreciate the high-quality ingredients, large portions, and respectable wine list. ⊛ Map M5 • Rua Barão da Torre 600, Ipanema • (021) 2512 2970 • $$$$$

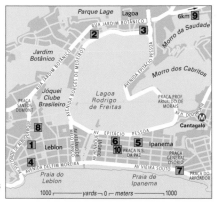

Academia da Cachaça's liquors

Bars and Nightclubs

1 Academia da Cachaça
This informal streetside bar has one of the best selections of Brazil's national drink in the city. *Cachaça* is distilled from sugar-cane and is the basis of *caipirinha* cocktails. The bar is liveliest on Friday evenings. ◈ *Map L5 • Rua Conde de Bernadotte 26G, Leblon • (021) 2239 1542*

2 Baronneti
One of the most fashionable night spots in southern Rio de Janeiro, this restaurant-lounge-club's interior is very stylish, with plain white tones and mood lighting. Come midnight, a young, stylish crowd descends on the club downstairs. ◈ *Map N5 • Rua Barão da Torre 354, Ipanema • (021) 2247 9100*

3 Mistura Fina
Original *bossa nova* acts *(see p38)* from the 1960s and smaller, jazz-influenced international artists play at this sophisticated restaurant-cum-jazz

Mistura Fina

Rio Scenarium

bar between Copacabana and Ipanema beaches. There is a piano bar for pre-show drinks and light meals. ◈ *Map Q6 • Av Rainha Elizabeth Bélgica 770, Ipanema • (021) 2523 1703*

4 Rio Scenarium
Lapa's plushest *samba* venue hosts live acts downstairs that play standards like *Aquarela do Brasil*, while the club upstairs plays more contemporary Brazilian dance music. There is plenty of quieter sitting space in the gallery areas *(see p84)*.

5 Carioca da Gema
Arguably Rio's best live *samba* club, Carioca da Gema is housed in an intimate, converted two-story town house in Lapa, a short stroll from Rio Scenarium. Some of the best old *samba* and *choro* acts in the city

Botequim *or boteco bars are Rio institutions and always serve light food as well as draught beer (see p60). Bar Luíz is typical.*

play here. It is a very popular venue and gets crowded on weekends, so come early to ensure you get a table or bar space (see p84).

Bardot
A bar on the most fashionable dining street in Leblon, Bardot

Bar Luíz

attracts a swish set on weekends, but is very quiet during the week. Crowds can dance to modern club music on the intimate dance floor. ⊗ Map K5
• Rua Dias Ferreira 247a, Leblon
• (021) 2274 5590

Nuth
This mock-Miami, split-level dance club lies in Barra da Tijuca, half an hour from Ipanema. You can enjoy cocktails in the garden or dance to Eurotrash sounds on the packed dance floor. Visit on weekends after 11pm. ⊗ Map B6
• Av Armando Lombardi 999, Barra da Tijuca
• (021) 3575 6850 • www.nuth.com.br

Melt
The dance floor in this no-frills club gets so packed on weekends that it is almost impossible to move. Come before 10pm for a drink in the lower lounge bar. Melt often hosts live bands playing great Rio samba funk.
⊗ Map K6 • Rua Rita Ludolf 47, Leblon
• (021) 2249 9309

00
Stylish and eclectic, 00 (pronounced "zero zero") offers a

mixed program of live music and DJs. The little cocktail bar spills into a garden, so it is always possible to find a quiet spot away from the music (see p106).

Bar Luíz
This long bar-restaurant, with its busy black-tie waiters, has long been an after-work institution in Rio. Famous Cariocas, including Heitor Villa-Lobos (see p68), used to come here for a chopp (draught beer), petiscos (tapas), and conversation, as his modern-day counterparts still do, especially on Friday evenings (see p62).

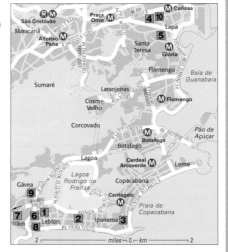

Left **Baixo Bebê** Right **Capuchin monkeys at the Parque Nacional do Itatiaia**

🔟 Activities for Children

1 Jardim Zoológico

As well as housing over 2,000 animals, including large carnivores in big enclosures, this smart, modern zoo runs an important captive-breeding programme for marmosets and tamarins – the world's smallest monkeys. A little train takes children through the zoo. Ⓝ *Map E1 • Quinta da Boa Vista, São Cristóvão • (021) 3878 4200 • Open 9am–4:30pm Tue–Sun • Adm • www.rio. rj.gov.br/web/riozoo*

2 Jardim Botânico

Tucked away behind Lagoa Rodrigo de Freitas, this shady tropical garden, with its ponds, little streams, and waterfalls, is a lovely place to while away a sunny afternoon. Children will be delighted to spot squirrels and *agoutis* – rabbit-sized rodents that look a little like tiny deer. The garden's Café Botânico sells ice cream *(see pp18–19)*.

A waterfall in Jardim Botânico

3 Sugar Loaf Mountain

The views from the Sugar Loaf and Morro da Urca may be spectacular, but children will particularly relish the dramatic cable-car rides to the hilltops. The trails on the hills are also worth exploring. Look out for the indigenous tufted-eared marmosets. The Sugar Loaf has a café-bar and Morro da Urca has cafés and restaurants, as well as a theater that hosts popular shows and concerts *(see pp12–13)*.

4 Baixo Bebê

This little playground, tucked under the looming Os Dios Irmãos hill at the far end of Leblon beach, has climbing frames and sandpits. Kids can cool off with coconut milk available at juice stalls nearby. There are child-friendly cafés and restaurants too. This is one of Leblon's safest areas. Ⓝ *Map L6 • Leblon beach*

5 Espaço Cultural da Marinha

The Navy Cultural Center features a museum of underwater archaeology and navigation, and ships moored in a private harbor. *Galeota*, a former royal barge that is used for tours around the bay, a submarine, and a World War II warship – the Bauru – will also fascinate youngsters. Ⓝ *Map X2 • Av Alfredo Agache, Centro • (021) 2233 9165 • Open noon–5pm Tue–Sun • www.mar.mil.br/ dphdm/ecm/ecm_loc.htm*

A powerful telescope at the Planetário

6 Planetário

This state-of-the-art planetarium is one of the best of its kind in South America. As well as astronomical shows (narrated in Portuguese), it has an interesting museum that features touch displays. Kids of all ages are permitted to use the powerful telescopes to view planets and galaxies three times a week *(see p74)*.

7 Rio Water Planet

The largest collection of water slides, pools, and rides in Rio state are found in Rio Water Planet in the suburb of Vargem Grande, some 12 miles (20 km) from the city center. The best way to visit is by car or taxi as public transport is limited. ◉ *Map A6*
• *Estrada dos Bandeirantes, Vargem Grande* • *(021) 2428 9000* • *Open 10am–5pm Sat–Sun; closed in winter* • *Adm* • *www. riowaterplanet.com.br*

8 Parque da Catacumba

This lushly forested, hilly park overlooking Lagoa has a zip-wire adventure trail from raised platforms suspended in the trees. There are different levels suitable for adults and children – all are great fun. Entrance to the park is free, but there is a small charge for the zip-wire trail *(see p73)*.

9 Helicopter Tours

Helicopters leave from Lagoa Rodrigo de Freitas, Morro da Urca, and the Mirante Dona Marta near Corcovado, and chart a course over the city's beaches and spectacular natural monuments *(see p53)*.

10 Parque Nacional do Itatiaia

Protecting a large area of rain forest, Brazil's first national park is ideal for wildlife spotting. Capuchin monkeys and coatis are common sights on the trails that lead through the forest near the hotels, or off the park road. The park is also good for bird-watching, as it has about 250 bird species *(see p96)*.

Left **Beach volleyball** Right **Hiking in Parque Nacional de Tijuca**

🔟 Sports and Outdoor Activities

1 Running
Jogging in the early morning or late afternoon is a favorite Carioca pastime. The best places for running are Copacabana, Ipanema, and Leblon.

2 Beach Volleyball
Ipanema and Copacabana beach are popular spots to play this game. CBV offers beach volleyball classes with all equipment provided. 🅢 *CBV: Map L6 • Rua Carlos Góis, Leblon • (021) 8117 3998 • Adm for classes • www.beachvolleyballrio.com*

3 Surfing
The best beaches to surf in Rio city are in Ipanema and Leblon – especially at Arpoador beach. Boards can be rented through a school, such as Rico Surf. 🅢 *ricosurf.globo.com • Adm*

4 Kite Surfing
The waves and strong winds to the east of Rio city, beyond Niterói, make this one of the top places for kite surfing. Surfers are attached to kites and dragged through the waves. The best place to learn the sport is in Cabo Frio town, which is 93 miles (148 km) east of Rio. 🅢 *Extreme Sports Café: Map C2 • Praia do Foguete • www.extremesportscafe.com • Adm*

Surfer at Arpoador beach

5 Windsurfing
Windsurfing is excellent to the east of Rio, where lagoons and high winds make conditions ideal. MGW Tours offers windsurfing in Niterói. 🅢 *Map C2 • www.mgwbrasil.com.br*

6 Hang Gliding and Paragliding
There are few locations more spectacular for these sports than Rio. Flights launch from the Pedra Bonita *(see p11)* and land at São Conrado beach. Numerous companies offer flights. 🅢 *Adm • www.justflyinrio.blogspot.com*

7 Hiking
The hilly, forested terrain around Rio offers great walking opportunities. One of the best hikes is to the summit of the

Paragliding

Rock climbing

Pedra da Gávea *(see p11)*, the world's tallest coastal monolith.
🖱 *www.trilhasrj.com.br*

8 Rock Climbing

Rio has many great rock climbs and the views and locations are fabulous. Top of the list are the Sugar Loaf and Morro da Urca *(see pp12–13)*. Other equally beautiful but lesser-known locations include Parque Nacional do Itatiaia *(see p96)* and the Serra dos Órgãos *(see p95)*.
🖱 *www.climbinrio.com*

9 Golf

The best golf course in Rio is in Gávea. The 18-hole club is private, but games can be booked through concierges at the better Rio hotels. 🖱 *Gávea Golf and Country Club: Map D6 • Estrada da Gávea 800, São Conrado • (021) 3323 6050 • Adm*

10 Diving

Intensive factory fishing in the 1980s has damaged some of the marine life in the waters around Rio. There are still some reasonable dive sites at Arraial do Cabo, near Cabo Frio *(see p96)*, where there is a wealth of soft corals, sponges, and marine life. 🖱 *Map C2*

Top 10 Surf Beaches

1 Arpoador
The best surf is near the rocks at the north of Ipanema. Be careful of the undertow.

2 Leblon
Although the waves here are easy for beginners, the current can be strong and the water is icy.

3 Prainha
The most powerful waves in Rio pound this beach in the far south – beyond Recreio dos Bandeirantes.

4 Barra
This 11-mile (18-km) stretch of sand is one of the most popular for surfing and offers good beach breaks.

5 Recreio
At the end of Recreio beach is Surfers' Point. Waves on this long beach break at rocks a few meters from the shore.

6 São Conrado
The surf here varies but there are usually beach breaks of between 3 and 5 ft (1 and 1.5 m). Hang gliders usually land here in the afternoons.

7 Grumari
The biggest waves in Rio hit Prainha and this beach just to its south, which tends to be quiet during the week.

8 Barra da Guaratiba
This river mouth near Prainha is pounded by perfectly formed, powerful waves – great for surfing.

9 Itaipu
This is one of the most popular beaches in the area for surfing, body boarding, and windsurfing.

10 Itacoatiara
Some of the best waves in Rio state hit this beach just east of Niterói.

Left **Helicopter tour** Center *Favela* **art exhibit** Right **Beach buggy tour**

Tours and Excursions

1 Favela Tour
A visit to one of Rio's *favelas* (see p74) is an eye-opening experience that challenges common preconceptions about such poor areas. Only visit with an operator who contributes to the community. Ⓢ *Adm • www.favelatour.org, www.favelatour.com.br*

2 Walking Tour
A guided walking tour is the best way to see the historic sights of the center and Santa Teresa, but beware of snatch thefts on the way. Ⓢ *Adm • www.culturalrio.com.br*

3 Soccer at Estádio do Maracanã
The crowd at the world's largest soccer stadium is wild. Watch Rio–São Paulo derbies or an international game. Tour operators offer visits (see p35).

4 Hiking in and around Rio
Rio Hiking offers treks in Parque Nacional da Tijuca. It also covers the Serra dos Órgãos (see p95) and Parque Nacional do Itatiaia (see p96), with various routes through the rain forest. Ⓢ *Adm • www.riohiking.com.br*

5 Jeep and Buggy Tours
Jeep tours through Parque Nacional da Tijuca and around the city are very popular. Beach buggy tours take in Corcovado, Tijuca, and the Sugar Loaf, and offer a more personal experience. Ⓢ *Adm • www.jeeptour.com.br*

6 Walks up Corcovado
Among the walks offered by Rio Trilhas, the best is a half-day trip along a trail from Parque Lage (see p75) to Corcovado (see pp8–9). Ⓢ *Map D4 • www.riotrilhas.com.br*

Crowds going wild at a soccer match at Maracanã

Hikers in Parque Nacional da Tijuca

7 Guanabara Bay Boat Tours
Though polluted, Guanabara Bay is one of the world's most beautiful natural harbors. Views of Rio from the water are magical. ◈ Adm • www.saveiros.com.br

8 Helicopter Tours
A helicopter trip over Rio takes in Corcovado, the Sugar Loaf, the ocean beaches, and Maracanã. Views are best in the middle of the day as the shadows are at their shortest (see p12). ◈ Adm • www.helisight.com.br

9 Luxury Cruises Around Paraty and Ilha Grande
The coast between Rio and São Paulo is studded with rain forest-covered islands and mountain spurs. Angatu offers luxury cruises on yachts and motor cruisers in the region, with the option of homestays at private beach houses. ◈ Adm • www. angatu.com

10 Private Drive Tours to Petrópolis and Around
Hire a driver and private vehicle to visit the mountains behind Rio. Flecked with national parks and colonial towns, the area includes the Serra dos Órgãos and the imperial summer capital, Petrópolis, which has many palaces and stately buildings. ◈ Adm

Top 10 Viewpoints

1 Sugar Loaf Mountain
Visit in the morning for golden sun-lit views over Guanabara Bay and Corcovado (see pp12–13).

2 Corcovado
Best visited in the late afternoon when the Sugar Loaf and Guanabara Bay are a deep orange-yellow (see pp8–9).

3 Pedra da Gávea
As can be expected, the views from the world's highest coastal monolith are lovely (see p11).

4 Museu Casa Benjamin Constant
The garden of this museum offers wonderful views of the city center (see p82).

5 Niterói
This city across Guanabara Bay offers fabulous views of Rio (see p36).

6 Parque Lage
The glimpses from here through the forest to Corcovado and Cristo Redentor are breathtaking (see p75).

7 Praia de Ipanema
At sunset the beach is drenched in rich golden light and Os Dois Irmãos mountains form beautiful silhouettes (see p36).

8 Rocinha Favela
This favela on the hills boasts some of the finest views of the city (see p74).

9 Floresta da Tijuca
Tijuca watches out over almost all of central Rio and offers great views. ◈ Map D4

10 Flights into Rio
Planes coming into Aeroporto Santos Dumont (see p103) spectacularly swoop over the bay. ◈ Map J2

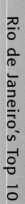

Left **Garcia and Rodrigues** Center **One of Getúlio's model trams** Right **Casa Turuna's costumes**

Shopping

1 Arts and Crafts from the Feira Hippie Market

There is overpriced bric-a-brac in this well-known market in central Ipanema, but also the occasional gem. Look for models of Rocinha houses made of wood or papier-mâché and illuminated from within, and for rope sculptures made by a *favela* artist *(see p90)*.

2 Northeastern Arts and Crafts from Feira de São Cristóvão

It is as much worth coming to this vast, bustling market for the *forró* music and the spectacle, as it is for the arts and crafts and delicious northeastern food. ⊛ *Map E1* • *Centro Luiz Gonzaga de Tradições Nordestinos, Campo de São Cristóvão* • *(021) 2580 0501* • *Open 10am–4pm Tue–Thu and non-stop 10am Fri–10pm Sun* • *www.feiradesaocristovao.org.br*

O Boticário sign

Arts and crafts at the Feira Hippie Market

3 Perfume from O Boticário

O Boticário is a Brazilian chain of cosmetic and body-care shops, similar to The Body Shop, found all over the city. It has a range of superior natural products including tasteful perfumes and aftershaves, many of which are made from scents derived from Brazilian plants. ⊛ *Map W3* • *www.oboticario.com.br*

4 Bikinis from Lenny

The only place in Rio that has a dress code is the beach. Unless you want to be recognized as a tourist, it is best to wear what the locals wear. Brazilian swimwear is widely regarded as the most fashionable in the world – at least by fashionistas and models – and the best place to find the most trendy cuts and patterns is in the heart of Ipanema, at Lenny. There are many other stores nearby, including Salinas and Blue Man. ⊛ *Map N5* • *Rua Visconde de Pirajá 351 Loja 114/115, Ipanema* • *(021) 2523 3796* • *www.lenny.com.br*

5 Coffee from Garcia and Rodrigues

This swanky bakery and coffee shop serves light meals, salads, and great coffee. The coffee is also available to buy ground to take home. ⊛ *Map B6* • *Barra Shopping, Av das Américas 4666* • *(021) 2431 8840* • *www.garciaerodrigues.com.br*

6 Jewelry from Antônio Bernardo

Brazil's most stylish, exclusive jeweler has branches worldwide, but the best choice is still to be found in Brazil where it all began. This is the award-winning jeweler's flagship shop, where a pair of earrings can set you back $2,000. ✆ *Map M5 • Rua Garcia D'Avila, Ipanema • (021) 2512 7204 • www.antoniobernardo.com.br*

7 Music from Livraria da Travessa or Toca do Vinícius

The charming Livraria da Travessa offers a selection of Brazilian music DVDs and great coffee. Toca do Vinícius *(see p90)* in Ipanema is the place to go for traditional *samba*, *bossa nova*, and *choro* records. ✆ *Livraria da Travessa: Map N5 • Rua Visconde de Pirajá 572, Ipanema (one of seven branches) • (021) 3205 9002 • www.travessa.com.br*

8 Carnaval Costumes from Casa Turuna

Those wanting to take a bit of Carnaval color home or to dress themselves up during Carnaval week should head for this store in Centro. It sells everything from feather boas to sequin bikinis at very reasonable prices. ✆ *Map W2 • Rua Senhor dos Passos 122, Centro • (021) 2509 3908*

9 Model Trams from Getúlio

Growing up on the streets of Rio, Getúlio Damato started making and selling models of Santa Teresa trams. Today, his little tram-shaped

Antônio Bernardo's flagship shop, Ipanema

workshop is a much-loved local institution and his models are collectors' items. ✆ *Map W6 • Btwn Rua do Aqueducto and Francisco de Castro*

10 Parceria Carioca

This great shop sells fun and funky accessories and crafts made by local cooperatives in some of Rio's poorest neighborhoods. The proceeds help to fund artisan workshops. ✆ *Map E5 • Rua Jardim Botânico 728 • (021) 2259 1437 • www.parceriacarioca.com.br*

AROUND TOWN

Centro
58–63

The Guanabara Bay
Beach Neighborhoods
66–71

Lagoa, Gávea, and
Jardim Botânico
72–77

Santa Teresa and Lapa
80–85

Copacabana, Ipanema
and Leblon
86–91

Rio de Janeiro State
94–99

RIO DE JANEIRO'S TOP 10

Left **Igreja Santo Antônio** Right **Catedral Metropolitana de São Sebastião**

Centro

RIO'S BUSTLING CITY CENTER SITS ON A PROMONTORY *that juts out into Guanabara Bay, to the north of Sugar Loaf Mountain (see pp12–13). A wave of rash construction in the early 20th century led to many of the area's finest buildings being razed to the ground, and the center lost much of the architectural unity that characterizes many Latin American cities. However, reminders of Rio's grand past can still be found scattered around Centro's broad avenues, where unremarkable civic and commercial buildings are interspersed with delightful palaces and Baroque churches, as well as fascinating museums and art galleries.*

A monument on Praça XV

Sculptures on display at Museu Nacional de Belas Artes

🔟 Sights

1. Mosteiro de São Bento
2. Museu Nacional de Belas Artes
3. Museu Histórico Nacional
4. Praça XV
5. Igreja Santo Antônio
6. Catedral Metropolitana de São Sebastião
7. Candelária Church
8. Real Gabinete Português de Leitura
9. Confeitaria Colombo
10. Nossa Senhora da Lapa

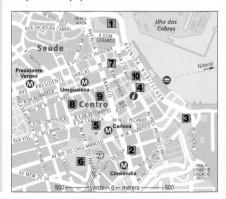

Previous pages **Praia de Copacabana**

1 Mosteiro de São Bento

Rio's oldest church is also one of Brazil's most beautiful. Its modest façade belies a lavish interior of Baroque carvings, including an opulent Blessed Sacrament Chapel. If you visit on Sundays at 10am, you can hear the Benedictine monks, who live in the adjacent monastery, singing a Latin mass (see pp14–15).

2 Museu Nacional de Belas Artes

Rio's foremost art gallery houses one of Latin America's most impressive collections. Vitor Meirelles' apology for colonialism, *A Primeira Missa no Brasil*, is displayed here. Arguably more interesting modernist Brazilian work is represented by painters such as Cândido Portinari, Emiliano Di Cavalcanti, and the *antropofagista* Tarsila do Amaral, who defined the modern Brazilian style (see pp16–17).

3 Museu Histórico Nacional

Devoted entirely to the history of Brazil, Museu Histórico Nacional is one of the largest museums in the country. Panels and displays trace the development of Brazil from the Stone Age, when the first inhabitants left paintings in the Serra da Capivara, up until the first days of the republic. A café next to the lobby serves delicious coffee, fresh juices, and snacks. Visit during the week to avoid the crowds (see pp20–21).

Blessed Heart altarpiece, Mosteiro de São Bento

4 Praça XV

Dominated by the Paço Imperial, this flagstone square next to the ferry port preserves the memory of Rio under Portuguese rule more than any other part of the city. Until the Proclamation of the Republic in 1889, this square was the political center of Rio and Minas Gerais, and after the arrival of the royal family, it was the seat of power for Brazil. Praça XV is home to historic buildings, restaurants, shops, and two of central Rio's finest churches – Igreja de Nossa Senhora do Monte do Carmo and Igreja da Ordem Terceira de Nossa Senhora Carmo da Antiga Sé (see pp22–3).

Rock paintings at the Museu Histórico Nacional

For museums and galleries in Centro **See pp34–5.**

Interior of Candelária Church

5 Igreja Santo Antônio

Rio's second-oldest convent is set in a series of beautiful colonial churches on a hill over-looking Largo da Carioca. The bright interior is decorated with tiles and statues of St. Anthony. Women are often seen praying to the saint, who is said to be a provider of husbands. ◎ Map W3 • Largo da Carioca s/n • (021) 2262 0129 • Open 7:30am–6:30pm Mon–Fri, 7:30–11:30am, 2:30–6pm Sat, 9:30–11:30am Sun

6 Catedral Metropolitana de São Sebastião

Often falsely attributed to Brazil's most famous modernist architect, Oscar Niemeyer *(see p68)*, the cathedral was actually built by Edgar de Oliveira da Fonseca in

Stained glass at Catedral Metropolitana

1976–84. The basement houses a Sacred Art Museum preserving age-old artifacts of the Portuguese royal family. ◎ Map W4 • Av República do Chile 245 • (021) 2240 2669 • Open 7am–6pm daily (museum 9am–noon Wed, Sat & Sun; also 1–4pm Wed) • www.catedral.com.br

7 Candelária Church

This grand Italianate temple has long been the church of choice for high-society Rio. Built between 1775 and 1894, the church was modeled on Lisbon's Basilica de Estrela; the marble for the interior was shipped from Verona. The Candelária gets its name from a chapel built in homage to Our Lady of Candles, which stood on the same site from 1610. ◎ Map W2 • Praça Pio X • (021) 2233 2324 • Open 8am–4pm Mon–Fri, 8am–noon Sat, 9am–1pm Sun

8 Real Gabinete Português de Leitura

This splendid library is a hidden treasure in the city center. The Manueline style evolved in Portugal in the 15th century and is unique because of its Islamic influences and nautical motifs. The library was built in the 19th century by the Portuguese architect Rafael da Silva e Castro, and is thought to house the biggest

collection of Portuguese literary works outside Portugal.
👁 Map W3 • Rua Luís de Camões 30 • (021) 2221 3138 • Open 9am–6pm Mon–Fri • www.realgabinete.com.br

9 Confeitaria Colombo

This excellent bakery-tea house is few blocks from the Real Gabinete. The lower gallery features towering mirrors, while the upper gallery is brightened by a delightful Art Nouveau skylight. The *feijoada (see p110)* colonial lunch on Saturdays is often accompanied by live music. There is another branch of Confeitaria Colombo at Forte de Copacabana *(see p25)*. 👁 Map W2 • Rua Gonçalves Dias 32 • (021) 2505 1500 • Open 9am–8pm Mon–Fri, 9:30am–5pm Sat • www.confeitariacolombo.com.br

Lavish interior of the Confeitaria Colombo

10 Nossa Senhora da Lapa

The modest exterior of this little church tucked away near Praça XV belies its stunning Baroque interior. The dome, which is illuminated by a series of round windows and an oval skylight, is particularly lovely. The church is a haven of peace in the bustle of central Rio. 👁 Map X2 • Rua do Ouvidor 35 • (021) 2509 2339 • Open 8am–2pm Mon–Fri

A Day in the Historic Center

Morning

🕐 Begin with a visit to a temporary exhibition in the **Paço Imperial** *(see p22)* or the fine churches that cluster around nearby **Praça XV** *(see p22)*. There is often some interesting bric-a-brac in the little market on the square and the shop inside the **Paço Imperial** is great for browsing. Walk north across the square under the **Arcos de Teles** archway and along the charming **Travessa do Comércio** *(see p23)*. Visit **Nossa Senhora da Lapa** on the corner and turn left onto Rua Ouvidor toward Avenida Rio Branco. The streets off Ouvidor throng with activity and give a real feel of Rio's working life. Next, take a left onto Rua Gonçalves Dias and have lunch at the **Confeitaria Colombo** at number 32.

Afternoon

The magnificent **Real Gabinete Português de Leitura** is close by. To reach it, walk back up Rua Gonçalves Dias and turn left onto Rua Ouvidor – it is just after the São Francisco de Paula church on the right. Then head south along Rua Ramalho Ortigão to the Largo da Carioca and the Baroque **Igreja Santo Antônio**, which is on a hill. You will see the cone of **Catedral Metropolitana de São Sebastião** from here. The **Teatro Municipal** *(see p63)* is east along Avenida República do Chile. From here it is a stroll across Avenida Rio Branco to the **Museu Nacional de Belas Artes** *(see pp16–17)* or the **Amarelinho** *boteco (see p62)* for a *chopp* beer.

Left **Confeitaria Colombo** Right **Bar Luíz**

Botecos and Cafés

1 Adega do Timão
Decorated with nautical relics and illuminated by a 19th-century French chandelier, this bar attracts a lively after-work crowd. ⊗ *Map W2 • Rua Visconde de Itaboraí 10 • (021) 2224 9616*

2 Confeitaria Colombo
This grand Portuguese coffee shop, which doubles up as a *boteco*, serves snacks as well as sweet cakes *(see p61)*.

3 Botecos on Travessa do Comércio
The *botecos* that line this alley by Praça XV *(see pp22–3)* are a favorite haunt for Cariocas in search of cold beer, tasty snacks, and great atmosphere. ⊗ *Map X2*

4 Amarelinho
This bright yellow *boteco* has been here since the early 20th century. The best tables have a partial view of the Sugar Loaf. ⊗ *Map X4 • Praça Floriano 55B • (021) 2240 8434*

5 Bar Luíz
Rio's most famous and celebrated *boteco* has been serving delicious German beer and snacks since 1887. ⊗ *Map W3 • Rua da Carioca 39 • (021) 2262 6900*

6 O Paladino
One of Centro's most traditional *botecos* often plays live music at night. Try the prawn *pestico*. ⊗ *Map W2 • Rua Uruguaiana 226 • (021) 2263 2094*

7 Botecos on Beco das Sardinhas
It is fun to wander around this bustling pedestrian street, sampling beers and snacks from its many *botecos* as you go. ⊗ *Map W2 • Rua Miguel Couto*

8 Belmonte Lapa
This fun and lively bar is popular with Lapa's young arty crowd. Try the ultra-chilled *chopp* draft beer with some tasty *petiscos* (tapas). ⊗ *Map W4 • Av Mem de Sá 90 • (021) 2224 2169*

9 Bar Brasil
This German *boteco* offers a broad range of Bavarian food and beer. The wall paintings are by the artist Selarón, who decorated the Ladeira de Selarón *(see pp82–3)*. ⊗ *Map W4 • Av Mem de Sá 90 • (021) 2509 5943*

10 Rio Minho
Excellent seafood is on offer in this *boteco*-restaurant, which is famous for its loyal clientele. Many working Cariocas visit during lunchtime. ⊗ *Map W2 • Rua do Ouvidor 10 • (021) 2509 2338*

To find out more about botecos **See p60**.

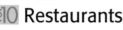

Price Categories

For a three-course meal for one with half a bottle of wine (or equivalent meal), taxes, and extra charges.	**$** under US$15
	$$ US$15–US$25
	$$$ US$25–US$35
	$$$$ US$35–US$50
	$$$$$ over US$50

Exterior of Albamar

🔟 Restaurants

1 Albamar
Once part of a large market that was demolished in 1933, this tower restaurant, which serves delicious seafood, was so popular with Rio's high society that it survived. ◈ *Map X2 • Praça Marechal Âncora • (021) 2240 8378 • $$$$*

2 Café do Theatro
This popular lunchtime spot offers excellent coffee, cakes, and light snacks. ◈ *Map X3 • Theatro Municipal, Av Rio Branco • (021) 2262 3935 • Closed for dinner • $*

3 Brasserie Europa
Executives come here to lunch in air-conditioned comfort on weekdays over ice-cold beers. ◈ *Map W4 • Rua Senador Dantas 117 • (021) 2220 2656 • $$*

4 Bistro do Paço
Located in the central atrium of the Paço Imperial (see p22), this café-restaurant has a menu of light lunches. ◈ *Map X2 • Paço Imperial, Praça XV • (021) 2262 3613 • $$*

5 Cais do Oriente
The Cais, one of Centro's most lavish restaurants, serves Brazilian versions of Asian and Mediterranean dishes. ◈ *Map X2 • Rua Visconde de Itaboraí 8 • (021) 2233 2531 • $$*

6 Cria da Terra
Healthy sandwiches and snacks are the draw at this buffet restaurant. ◈ *Map W2 • Rua Sete de Setembro 48 • (021) 2242 9009 • $$*

7 Mosteiro
Named in honor of the nearby Mosteiro de São Bento (see pp14–15), this traditional restaurant is famous for its *bacalhau* (salted cod). ◈ *Map W1 • Rua São Bento 13/15 • (021) 2233 6426 • $$$$*

8 Margutta Citta
This great restaurant offers Italian fish dishes, pasta, and risottos. These are served in a bright, airy dining room, and service is crisp. ◈ *Map X4 • Av Graça Aranha 1 • (021) 2563 4091 • $$$$*

9 Al-Kuwait
The menu at this immensely popular and good-value Arabic and North African restaurant also includes some Brazilian fare. ◈ *Map X4 • Av Treze de Maio 23 • (021) 2240 1114 • $$*

10 Bistrô dos Correios
Tucked inside the Centro Cultural Dos Correios and handy for its exhibitions, this smart little bistro is good for lunch and delicious afternoon teas. ◈ *Map X2 • Rua Visconde de Itaboraí 20 • (021) 2219 5324 • Open noon–7pm • $$*

Left **Museu de Folclore Edison Carneiro** Right **Museu Carmen Miranda**

The Guanabara Bay Beach Neighborhoods

RIO DE JANEIRO STRETCHES SOUTH *into Guanabara Bay through a series of magnificent beach neighborhoods, which reach the Sugar Loaf at the mouth of the bay. The history of fashionable Rio can be traced through these areas. In colonial times the aristocracy frequented Centro. Then they moved to Glória, with its yacht-filled harbor and, in the mid-20th century, to Flamengo and Botafogo. When the water became polluted they abandoned these for the Atlantic and Copacabana. Today Ipanema and Leblon are the popular places to live. However, the bay neighborhoods retain stately buildings, attractive parks, and interesting little museums and galleries.*

Sugar Loaf Mountain and Morro da Urca from Botafogo beach

🔟 Sights

1. Sugar Loaf Mountain
2. Monumento Nacional aos Mortos da II Guerra Mundial (War Memorial)
3. Igreja Nossa Senhora da Glória do Outeiro
4. Museu Carmen Miranda
5. Museu de Folclore Edison Carneiro
6. Museu do Índio
7. Museu Villa-Lobos
8. Praia de Fora
9. Pista Cláudio Coutinho
10. Casa de Rui Barbosa

Previous pages **Sugar Loaf Mountain at sunset**

Sugar Loaf Mountain

This famous peak sits in Guanabara Bay, staring out toward Niterói and the inky blue Atlantic. The view from the top is as breathtaking as from Cristo Redentor and looks best in the early morning. Although indigenous Brazilians have been scaling this rock for centuries, the first European reached the summit in 1817. Nowadays it is far easier to get there – by cable car, helicopter, or trail *(see pp12–13)*.

Monumento Nacional aos Mortos da II Guerra Mundial (War Memorial)

This beautifully balanced plinth supports two concrete columns topped by a convex slab, and is one of Rio's most impressive Modernist monuments. Often attributed to Oscar Niemeyer *(see p68)*, it was designed by architects Marcos Konder Neto and Hélio Ribas Marinho in 1952 to commemorate the Brazilian soldiers who were killed in fighting in Italy during World War II. ◎ *Map X5 • Av Infante Dom Henrique s/n, Glória • (021) 2240 1283 • Open 10am–4pm Tue–Sun*

War Memorial in Glória

Igreja Nossa Senhora da Glória do Outeiro

Igreja Nossa Senhora da Glória do Outeiro

One of the prettiest 18th-century churches in Rio lies just to the south of the War Memorial. It is perched on a little hill surrounded by woods, and overlooks the bay. The polygonal interior, lined with very fine painted blue and white *azulejo* tiles, is impressive. The church was the favorite of the Brazilian royal family. Emperor Dom Pedro II *(see p31)* was baptized here. ◎ *Map X6 • Praça Nossa Senhora da Glória 135, Glória • (021) 2225 0735 • Open 9am–noon and 1–5pm Tue–Fri, 9am–noon Sat & Sun • Adm*

Museu Carmen Miranda

A handful of relics from the first international Brazilian singing star are housed in this ungainly building shaped like a concrete pill box. On display are photos, costumes, newspaper cuttings, and magazine covers. Although Carmen lived in the city as a child and a teenager, she was born in Lisbon and her version of "being Brazilian" is generally regarded as a caricature. ◎ *Map H4 • Parque do Flamengo, moving to the new Museu da Imagem on Av Atlántica in 2014 • (021) 2334 4293 • Open 10am–5pm Tue–Fri, 1–5pm Sat–Sun • Adm*

Modernist Architecture and Oscar Niemeyer

The Palácio Gustavo Capanema *(see p70)* was the first Modernist building in the Americas. Oscar Niemeyer, who helped design it, became the most eminent Modernist architect in Latin America. However, his socialist views led to his exile in 1966. He returned in 1985 and continued to build. He died in 2012, aged 104.

5 Museu de Folclore Edison Carneiro

Displaying arts and crafts from all over Brazil, this museum features carved models and tableaus of rodeos, circuses, and festival scenes, which, when switched on, work like music boxes. Over 14,000 exhibits, including bibliographic documents, audiovisual displays, and hundreds of ceramic objects and photographs, paint a vivid picture of Brazil's cultural life. ◎ Map H3 • Rua do Catete 179–181, Catete • (021) 2285 0441 • Open 11am–6pm Tue–Fri, 3–6pm Sat, Sun & holidays

6 Museu do Indio

When the Europeans arrived, Brazil was inhabited by over 5 million indigenous people divided into at least 1,000 groups. Much of their culture was wiped out with the onset of slavery. This museum displays many indigenous objects and has rooms devoted to information panels and slide shows. There is also a *Guaraní maloca* (communal thatch house), a gift shop, and a library. ◎ Map Q1 • Rua das Palmeiras 55, Botafogo • (021) 3214 8702 • Open 9am–5:30pm Tue–Fri, 1–5pm Sat–Sun • Adm (free on Sun) • www.museudoindio.gov.br

7 Museu Villa-Lobos

Heitor Villa-Lobos is Latin America's most highly respected classical composer. Between 1917 and his death in 1959, he produced over 1,000 highly original works influenced by both foreign composers and Brazilian musical styles, particularly *choro*. His best-known piece is the *Bachianas Brasileiras*, which pays homage to both Bach and Brazilian folk music. The museum in the musician's former home is devoted to displays of his personal effects. These include many of his musical instruments, manuscripts, and recordings. The museum also hosts regular performances of his music. ◎ Map Q1 • Rua Sorocaba 200, Botafogo • (021) 2266 3845 • Open 10am–5pm Mon–Fri • www.museuvillalobos.org.br

8 Praia de Fora

This fabulous beach is huddled between the base of the Morro Cara de Cão and the Sugar Loaf. It was here that Estácio de Sá and his men disembarked on 1st March 1565, and founded the city of São Sebastião do Rio de Janeiro. It is regarded as one of the safest beaches in Rio and is popular with young, upper middle-class Cariocas, many of whom have weekend parties on the sand. ◎ Map J4 • Urca

Communal thatch house at the Museu do Indio

Casa de Rui Barbosa

9 Pista Cláudio Coutinho
This walking track snakes its way around the base of the Sugar Loaf and Morro da Urca, and then up to the top of Morro da Urca. The views are wonderful throughout. The trail cuts through woodland filled with tiny, tufted-eared marmosets and brilliantly colored tanagers, and dips onto the Praia de Fora beach. Walks are coolest in the early morning and the trail is one of the safest in urban Rio because of the huge army presence in Urca. ✆ Map J4
• Open 6am–6pm daily

10 Casa de Rui Barbosa
Rui Barbosa was one of the most influential politicians in the early years of the republic. His former home, one of many stately 19th-century town houses to have been preserved in Botafogo, is now a museum. There are often free concerts of classical music in the main hall and the gardens are an oasis of peace and quiet away from the bustle of Botafogo. ✆ Map Q1
• Rua Sao Clemente 134, Botafogo
• (021) 3289 4600 • Open 10am–6pm Tue–Fri, 2–6pm Sat–Sun and hols • Adm
• www.casaruibarbosa.gov.br

A Climb Up Morro da Urca and the Sugar Loaf

The sides of the twin boulder mountains of **Morro da Urca** and the **Sugar Loaf** (see pp12–13) look impossibly steep. But there is an easy path leading to the summit of Urca and a more challenging trail to the top of the **Sugar Loaf**. The trail at the foot of Urca is known as the **Pista Cláudio Coutinho**. This is guarded by a small gateway which is opened between 7am and 8am every morning. Look for the signpost at the eastern end of Praia Vermelha in Urca. The flat, paved path winds around the base of the **Sugar Loaf,** right next to the indigo water of Guanabara Bay. After about 330 yards (300 m) a signpost leads the way up the steep mountainside to the top of Urca. Steps soon give way to a bare trail, thick with creepers and roots. Before long it becomes possible to see right across Guanabara Bay to the city center. The summit of Urca takes about an hour to reach from the start. Bring plenty of water, a camera, sun protection, and a hat. Cool off beneath the trees or in the cafés at the top of **Morro da Urca**. The path up the **Sugar Loaf** is more difficult to access, and some stretches must be climbed. It is possible to climb the mountain with a tour company like **Rio Hiking** (see p52). It usually takes around two hours to reach the summit.

Left **Parque do Flamengo** Right **Fortaleza de São João**

🔟 Best of the Rest

1 Palácio Gustavo Capanema
The first modernist building in the Americas is on the list for UNESCO World Heritage Site consideration. ⊗ *Map X3 • Rua da Imprensa 16, Cinelândia • (021) 2220 1490 • Visits for groups only, by appointment*

2 Chafariz da Glória
Built in 1772, this is one of the city's oldest public-drinking fountains. It has been restored several times. ⊗ *Map X2 • Praça XV*

3 Memorial Getúlio Vargas
Brazil's authoritarian president lived in Rio for almost 30 years. These 50-ft (15-m) tall tapering marble columns sitting in an algae-filled pond remember him. ⊗ *Map X6 • Praça Luís de Camões, Glória • (021) 2245 7577 • Basement museum: open 10am–7pm Tue–Sun*

4 Marina da Glória
Boats leave from this harbor for tours around Guanabara Bay. Cruises usually take about four hours. ⊗ *Map X6 • Glória*

5 Castelinho do Flamengo
Romanesque, Art Nouveau, and Moorish unite in this odd-looking building, which houses a concert hall and arts center. ⊗ *Map H3 • Praia do Flamengo 158, Flamengo • (021) 2205 0655 • Open 10am–8pm Tue–Sat, 10am–6pm Sun*

6 Parque do Flamengo
Roberto Burle Marx landscaped these extensive gardens. There are wonderful views of the Sugar Loaf. ⊗ *Map H3 • Flamengo*

7 Casa de Arte e Cultura Julieta de Serpa
This Art Nouveau building houses a series of restaurants, bars, and exhibition spaces. ⊗ *Map H3 • Praia do Flamengo 340, Flamengo • (021) 2551 1278 • www.julietadeserpa.com.br*

8 Tempo Glauber
This museum, devoted to famous Brazilian director Glauber Rocha, features memorabilia and a private cinema. ⊗ *Map Q1 • Rua Sorocaba 190, Botafogo • (021) 2527 5840 • Open 11am–5pm Mon–Fri • Adm • www.tempoglauber.com.br*

9 Praia Vermelha
Located between the base of Morro da Urca and Morro da Babilônia, Praia Vermelha is home to two university campuses and a few military and navy buildings. ⊗ *Map J4 • Urca*

10 Fortaleza de São João
Estacio de Sá *(see p31)* founded this fort in 1565 in the Sugar Loaf's shadow. Only a Baroque gate of the original structure remains. ⊗ *Map J4 • Av João Luís Alves, Urca • (021) 2543 3323 • Open 9am–4pm Mon–Thu, 9am–noon Fri • Adm*

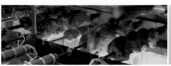

Price Categories

For a three-course meal for one with half a bottle of wine (or equivalent meal), taxes, and extra charges.

$	under US$15
$$	US$15–US$25
$$$	US$25–US$35
$$$$	US$35–US$50
$$$$$	over US$50

Porção Rio's mouth-watering cuisine

 # Places to Eat

1 Alcaparra
At this Portuguese-Italian restaurant, the risottos are popular, the deserts plentiful, and the wine list decent. ◈ Map H3 • Praia do Flamengo 150, Flamengo • (021) 2558 3937 • $$$$

2 Laguiole
Adventurous contemporary cuisine is the specialty at this restaurant in the Museu de Arte Moderna (see p35). ◈ Map X4 • Av Infante Dom Henrique 85 • (021) 2517 3129 • Open noon–5pm Mon–Fri • $$$$

3 Café Lamas
This street-corner snack bar has been serving steak and chips, bacalhau (salted cod), crème caramels, and juices since 1874. ◈ Map H3 • Rua Marques de Abrantes 18, Flamengo • (021) 2556 0799 • $$

4 Barracuda
This nautically themed seafood restaurant has grilled and fried fish as the house specialties. ◈ Map K6 • Av Infante Dom Henrique, Marina da Glória, Glória • (021) 2265 4641 • $$$$

5 Porção Rio's
This is one of the best churrascaria (steak houses) in Rio, so come with an empty stomach and without vegetarian friends. ◈ Map H3 • Av Infante Dom Henrique s/n, Flamengo s/n, Flamengo • (021) 3461 9020 • $$$$

6 Casa da Suíça
This Swiss restaurant has been serving cheese and meat fondues to Cariocas for 50 years. ◈ Map W5 • Rua Candido Mendes 157, Glória • (021) 2252 5182 • $$$$

7 Bon Vivant Bistrô e Delicatessen
This is a great bistro and delicatessen in the lower area of Botafogo. It serves delicious snacks and local delicacies. ◈ Map R1 • Rua Voluntários da Pátria 46, Botafogo • (021) 2537 2857 • Open for dinner daily • $$$

8 Yorubá
One of the best Bahian restaurants outside Salvador, Yorubá serves delightful seafood. ◈ Map Q1 • Rua Arnaldo Quintela 94, Botafogo • (021) 2541 9387 • $$$$

9 Raajmahal
Indian restaurants are hard to come by in Brazil, so savor the curry-house dishes on offer here. ◈ Map R1 • Rua General Polidoro 29, Botafogo • (021) 2542 6242 • $$$

10 Miam Miam
Light, flavorsome Mediterranean food and some of the finest caipirinhas in the city are served in this atmospheric brick-lined restaurant and mini-lounge bar. ◈ Map R1 • Rua General Goes Monteiro 34, Botafogo • (021) 2244 0125 • $$$$

Bahian cooking is widely considered to be the best in Brazil. It is spicy and based on seafood rather than red meat.

Left **Orchids at Jardim Botânico** Right **Parque Lage**

Lagoa, Gávea, and Jardim Botânico

THESE PROSPEROUS, UPPER-MIDDLE CLASS NEIGHBORHOODS *lie around Lagoa Rodrigo de Freitas, between Ipanema and Leblon, and Corcovado. They are the evening haunts of Rio's rich and fashionable, and the proximity of the TV Globo studios ensures that the numerous clubs, bars, and restaurants that dot the streets are always busy. Nightlife is at its wildest in Gávea, where the botecos around Praça Santos Dumont are particularly lively toward the weekends. There are myriad bars and watering holes around the lake too. During the day, shady parks and tropical gardens tempt visitors away from the beach.*

Pedal boats at Parque do Cantagalo

Sights

1. Jardim Botânico
2. Instituto Moreira Salles
3. Nightlife in Baixo Gávea
4. Parque da Catacumba
5. Largo do Boticário
6. Horto Florestal
7. Rocinha *Favela*
8. Planetário
9. Parque Lage
10. Parque do Cantagalo

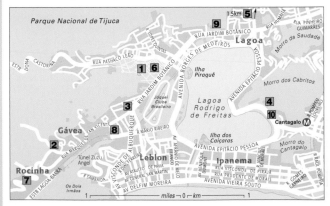

Jardim Botânico

There are 140 ha (348 acres) of broad, palm-tree-lined avenues, shady paths, and lawns dotted with classical fountains in these beautiful botanical gardens. Many of the trees here – like the *pau brasil*, for which the country was named – are threatened with extinction in the wild. Their branches and fruits and the tropical flowers that fill the garden attract birds and animals from the nearby Floresta da Tijuca. Allow at least three hours for a visit and come at the beginning of the day or after 3pm, when the temperatures are cooler *(see pp18–19).*

Sculpture in Parque da Catacumba

Instituto Moreira Salles

This attractive 19th-century house is set in lush grounds in front of a long blue pool. The gardens were landscaped by Roberto Burle Marx, one of the most important landscape architects of the 20th century. The colorful murals on the patio are the work of the famous Brazilian modernist painter, Cândido Portinari *(see p16).* The building

is now an exhibition space and has a little café serving excellent ground coffee and light food.
🔊 *Map D6 • Rua Marquês de São Vicente 476, Gávea • (021) 3284 7400 • Open 1–8pm Tue–Sun • www.ims.uol.com.br*

Nightlife in Baixo Gávea

The informal bars around Praça Santos Dumont in Baixo Gávea (the lower half of Gávea) fill with trendy Cariocas in the evenings from Thursday to Sunday. But since most tourists go out in Ipanema, Leblon, Copacabana, and Lapa, visitors are an anomaly here and are seldom left to sit alone. 🔊 *Map K4 • Praça Santos Dumont, Gávea*

Parque da Catacumba

Sculptures by Brazilian artists including Bruno Giorgi and Alfredo Ceschiatti (who made many of the monumental statues in Brasília) dot this wooded park opposite the Lagoa. A path leads to a 427-ft (130-m) high lookout with great views of Floresta da Tijuca and the beaches.
🔊 *Map N4 • Av Epitácio Pessoa 3,000 • (021) 2247 9949 • Open 8am–6pm daily • www.parquedacatacumba.com.br*

Murals at the Instituto Moreira Salles

→

Favelas

Most Cariocas live in slum cities – areas of poor-quality housing with little sanitation. Although most *favelas* are home to law-abiding people, many are plagued by gang violence. These communities have a rich cultural heritage – *samba*, Brazilian soccer, and Carnaval all began here. Only ever visit *favelas* on a guided tour *(see p52)*.

5 Largo do Boticário

This lovely square takes its name from Joaquim Luiz da Silva Souto, who was the pharmacist (*boticário*) to the royal family and lived here from 1831. The enclave, which boasts colonial-style buildings dating from the 1920s (some with picturesque *azulejos* – Portuguese tiles), cobbled streets, and a fountain, resembles a typical 19th-century Rio street. The square lies a little away from the Trêm do Corcovado funicular station in Cosme Velho, and can be accessed through the Rebouças tunnel. It is worth visiting en route to the famous statue of Cristo Redentor *(see p9)*. ◈ *Map G3*
• *Rua Cosme Velho 822, Cosme Velho*

6 Horto Florestal

This arboretum, located next to the Jardim Botânico, cultivates some 500 kinds of tropical trees, many of which are rare species from the Atlantic coastal rain forest. Saplings are sold here in an effort to encourage reforestation. ◈ *Map L3* • *Rua Pacheco Leão 2040, Jardim Botânico* • *(021) 3875 6211* • *Open 9–11am & 2–4pm Mon–Fri*

7 Rocinha Favela

The largest *favela* in Latin America takes its name from the little farm, or *rocinha*, that once stood on its now heavily urbanized hills teeming with some 150,000 people. The community here is served by its own local shops, TV and radio stations, restaurants, and bars. ◈ *Map D6*

8 Planetário

Gávea's stellar attraction, this complex features a museum of the universe, ultra-modern domes that can project thousands of stars onto their walls, and a viewing area, which offers stargazing sessions three times a week through powerful telescopes.

Façade of the Planetário

→

Rocinha, Rio's largest _favela_

🌐 Map K4 • Rua Vice-Governador Rubens Berardo 100, Gávea • (021) 2274 0046 • Open 9am–5pm Tue–Fri (3–5pm Dec–Mar), 3–6pm Sat & Sun; telescopes 6:30–8:30pm Tue–Thu (7:30am–9:30pm Dec–Mar) • Adm • www.rio.rj.gov.br/planetario

Parque Lage
An imposing, early-20th-century mansion, housing the School of Visual Art and fronted by Neo-Classical fountains, dominates this park. The house and gardens were designed by Englishman John Tyndale for a wealthy Carioca industrialist. The mansion's atrium now houses an arty café built around a water lily pond. Trails lead from the park to the summit of Corcovado and require a guide. 🌐 Map M2 • Rua Jardim Botânico 414, Jardim Botânico • (021) 3257 1800 • Open 8am–5pm daily

Parque do Cantagalo
This circular park winds around Lagoa Rodrigo de Freitas. There is a running track situated close to the water here, as well as cafés and bars where locals come to relax in the shade. Don't miss the swan-shaped pedal boats and kayaks that can be hired for a leisurely trip out onto the lake itself. 🌐 Map P4 • Parque do Cantagalo, Av Epitácio Pessoa s/n, Lagoa • (021) 2227 0837

A Day in Rio's Parks and Gardens

Morning

🕐 Start the day with a stroll around **Jardim Botânico** (see pp18–19). Try to arrive as close to 8am as possible and with binoculars in hand for the best chance to spot brilliantly colored birds like tanagers, cotingas, and numerous humming-birds, as well as small mammals like _paca_ and _agouti_. There is a kiosk at the entrance that gives out free maps of the gardens in a variety of languages, explaining where the important sights, including glass houses such as the **Orquidarium**, are situated. At about 11am, as the morning heats up, consider taking a helicopter flight out over **Corcovado** (see pp8–9) from the helipad just to the south of **Jardim Botânico**. The views of **Cristo Redentor** (see p9) are amazing.

Afternoon

🍴 Have lunch at one of the many kiosks overlooking **Lagoa Rodrigo de Freitas** on the eastern shore of the lake, which is in close proximity to the **Parque da Catacumba** (see p73). Drink plenty of juice or water and walk across Avenida Epitácio Pessoa for a 40-minute hike through the park, to the 427-ft- (130-m-) high look-out point at the Mirante do Sacopã. If there are no guards around, then be vigilant in the park or walk in a group. Head to **Parque Lage** by taxi for a pony ride or another light walk in the rain forest. ☕ Finish the afternoon with tea and biscuits in the mansion's atrium café.

Rio Hiking (www.riohiking.com) and Rio Trilhas (www.riotrilhas. com) offer walks from Parque Lage to Corcovado **See pp52–3.**

Left **Hipódromo Up** Center **Bar Lagoa** Right **Garota da Gávea**

🔟 Night Spots

1 Hipódromo Up
Filled with young Cariocas who come to mingle, this is a wonderful spot to meet the locals. ✎ *Map K4 • Praça Santos Dumont 108 • (021) 2274 9720*

2 Garota da Gávea
On weekends scores of people gather at this lively bar, just off Praça Santos Dumont, for *petiscos* (tapas) and drinks. ✎ *Map K4 • Praça Santos Dumont 148 • (021) 2274 2347*

3 Belmonte IV
Bakeries like Belmonte IV play an integral part in Brazil's nightlife, serving *empadas* (little stuffed filo pies) at all hours. ✎ *Map N2 • Rua Jardim Botânico 617 • (021) 2239 1649*

4 Caroline Café
This popular bar serves decent food and often has a DJ or live music after 11pm. ✎ *Map M3 • Rua JJ Seabra 10 • (021) 2540 0705*

5 Drink Café
Head to this lakeside bar for snacks and cocktails. There's good live music at weekends. ✎ *Map M4 • Kiosk 5, Av Borges de Medeiros • (021) 2239 4136*

6 Bar Jóia
This unpretentious and informal little street-corner bar attracts an eclectic young and local crowd at weekends and in the evenings. ✎ *Map M3 • Rua Jardim Botânico 594 • (021) 2539 5613*

7 Jota Bar
This well-liked bar attracts those looking for gourmet *petiscos*, which are some of the best in the city and come in sizes (and with prices) that befit a main course. ✎ *Map M2 • Rua Jardim Botânico 595 • (021) 2249 7437*

8 Saturnino
This bar-lounge has both outdoor and indoor areas and plays a variety of music. There is also a decent *caipirinha* and cocktail list. ✎ *Map M3 • Rua Saturnino de Brito 50 • (021) 3874 0064*

9 Bar Lagoa
Petiscos, light meals, and cocktails are on offer at Bar Lagoa, one of the oldest *botecos* in the area. There is also live music on most Fridays and weekends. ✎ *Map P5 • Av Epitácio Pessoa 1674 • (021) 2523 1135*

10 Palaphita Kitsch
The rustic log tables and chairs strewn under mock-Bedouin awnings and the strong *caipirinhas* on offer make this a favorite Carioca haunt. ✎ *Map P5 • Av Epitácio Pessoa, kiosk 20 • (021) 2227 0837*

Recommend your favorite bar on **traveldk.com**

Price Categories

For a three-course meal for one with half a bottle of wine (or equivalent meal), taxes, and extra charges.

\$	under US\$15
\$\$	US\$15–US\$25
\$\$\$	US\$25–US\$35
\$\$\$\$	US\$35–US\$50
\$\$\$\$\$	over US\$50

Braseiro da Gávea

 Restaurants

1 Guimas
Carioca celebrities lunch at this intimate, rustic restaurant, which serves traditional Portuguese and Brazilian cuisine. ✎ Map K4 • Rua José Roberto Macedo Soares 5 • (021) 2259 7996 • \$\$

2 66 Bistrô
Opened by Olympe's (see p44) chef Claude Troisgros, this French bistro has an affordable lunch buffet and classic French dishes. ✎ Map N2 • Av Alexandre Ferreira 66 • (021) 2266 0838 • \$\$\$

3 Café do Lage
Enjoy fresh-baked pastries and light lunches in a lovely open-air setting in the Parque Lage. ✎ Map F5 • Rua Jardim Botânico 414 • (021) 2226 8125 • No credit cards • \$\$

4 Arabe da Gávea
One of Rio's best Arabic restaurants bustles after dark. ✎ Map K4 • Rua Marquês de São Vicente 52, Shopping da Gávea • (021) 2294 2439 • \$\$

5 Les Artistes
This French restaurant-bar is popular with young Cariocas and becomes a club on Friday nights and weekends after 10pm. ✎ Map K4 • Rua Marquês de São Vicente 75 • (021) 2239 4242 • \$\$\$

6 Quadrifoglio
This chic Italian eatery is divided into a series of dining rooms, each with its own unique atmosphere. ✎ Map M3 • Rua J.J Seabra 19 • (021) 2294 1433 • \$\$

7 Pomodorino
Run by the owners of highly rated Artigiano, Pomodorino serves sublime Italian dishes and has a great selection of good-value wines. ✎ Map N5 • Av Epitácio Pessoa 1104 • (021) 3813 2622 • \$\$\$

8 Bacalhau do Rei
This family restaurant is frequented by Rio's Portuguese community and gets particularly busy on Sundays. ✎ Map K4 • Rua Marquês de São Vicente 11A • (021) 2239 8945 • \$\$\$

9 Braseiro da Gávea
Serving variations on the standard Brazilian meal of meat, fish, or poultry with beans, rice, or French fries, this restaurant is a popular meeting point for locals, especially on weekends. ✎ Map K4 • Praça Santos Dumont 116 • (021) 2239 7494 • \$\$\$

10 Mr Lam
With a partial view of Corcovado (see pp8–9), this vast, glass-walled Chinese restaurant is a stomping ground for affluent Cariocas. ✎ Map N2 • Rua Maria Angélica 21 • (021) 2286 6661 • \$\$\$\$

Left **Largo das Neves** Right **Detail of Escadaria Selarón**

Santa Teresa and Lapa

CHARMING ARCHITECTURE, COBBLED STREETS, *and a sense of community spirit give Santa Teresa, located on top of a hill overlooking Rio de Janeiro, an identity that is all its own. This unique character coupled with the superb panoramas out over Guanabara Bay and Centro have made the area popular with both tourists and locals. A tram and a series of brilliantly colored mosaic steps connect Santa Teresa with its neighbor, Lapa, at the foot*

of the hill. Not long ago, Lapa was a destitute area whose crumbling colonial buildings were home only to Rio's deprived. A renaissance that began in the late 1990s, inspired by the return of the Circo Voador music club, has transformed this district into the city's hottest nightspot. There is nowhere better for live Brazilian music than in the many botecos here, or beneath the Arcos da Lapa on Friday and Saturday nights.

A tram in Santa Teresa

🔟 Sights

1. Tram Rides
2. Largo das Neves
3. Largo dos Guimarães
4. Chácara do Céu
5. Museu Casa Benjamin Constant
6. Convento de Santa Teresa
7. Arcos da Lapa
8. Escadaria Selarón
9. Circo Voador
10. Feira do Antigo Rio

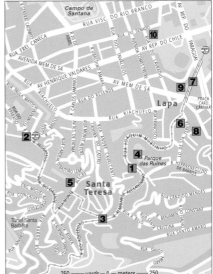

250 ⌐ yards ⌐ 0 ⌐ meters ⌐ 250

Previous pages **Escadaria Selarón**

Tram Rides

Trams are the best way to reach Santa Teresa from Centro. They jerk their way from a station next to the Catedral Metropolitana de São Sebastião *(see p60)*, across the Arcos da Lapa, and up the steep streets of Santa Teresa. The journey takes about 20 minutes and the trams are packed with colorful characters of all ages and backgrounds, many of whom are left precariously hanging onto the bars that run along the side of the tram. ◈ *Map V5 • Tram terminal: Rua Lélio Gama • (021) 2240 5709 • Trams run 6am–10pm daily • Adm*

Façade of Chácara do Céu

Largo das Neves

The smaller of Santa Teresa's two *praças* (town squares) is a great place to sit and watch the world go by. There are several *botecos* and restaurants here serving cold beer, pizza, and seafood dishes. It is the starting point of the Santa Teresa Carnaval parade *(see p40)*. ◈ *Map T5*

Largo dos Guimarães

Many of the neighborhood's best restaurants are clustered around this square,

including Espírito Santa *(see p84)* and Bar do Mineiro *(see p85)*. The area also features arts and crafts shops, and nearby, on Rua do Aqueducto, is a little yellow booth shaped like a tram, where the model trams found in many of Santa Teresa's restaurants are made by artisan Getúlio Damato *(see p55)*. ◈ *Map V6*

Chácara do Céu

The Chácara mansion, which has fantastic views over the city center, houses an exquisite museum featuring European and Asian art and antiques, as well as modern Brazilian works. Nearby is the Parque das Ruínas – the shell of another colonial mansion. ◈ *Map V5 • Rua Murtinho Nobre 93, Santa Teresa • (021) 3970 1126 • Open noon–5pm Wed–Mon • Adm (free Wed) • www.museuscastromaya.com.br*

Largo dos Guimarães

Museu Casa Benjamin Constant

This is the former home of Benjamin Constant, a political philosopher who led the republican movement and formulated key political ideas including the national motto, *Ordem e Progresso* (Order and Progress). The museum contains many personal items and offers great views. ⬡ Map U5 • Rua Monte Alegre 255, Santa Teresa • (021) 2509 1248 • Open 10am–5pm Wed–Fri, 1–5pm Sat & Sun • Adm

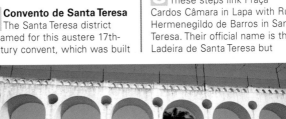

Museu Casa Benjamin Constant

Convento de Santa Teresa

The Santa Teresa district is named for this austere 17th-century convent, which was built in honor of St. Teresa – founder of the Discalced Carmelite order of the Catholic Church and disciple and friend of St. John of the Cross. Although much of this convent is closed to visitors, there is a small museum as well as access to the very spot where St. Teresa was born and the little garden where she used to play as a child. ⬡ Map W5 • Ladeira de Santa Teresa 52, Santa Teresa • (021) 2224 2040 • Open 7am–5pm Tue–Fri

Arcos da Lapa

Lapa is dominated by this aqueduct passing over Avenida Mem de Sá, which was built in 1724 to transport water from the Santa Teresa forest to the public drinking fountain near Largo da Carioca. Trams now run across the arches to and from Santa Teresa; lively bars and arts centers draw crowds to the adjoining square. ⬡ Map W4

Escadaria Selarón

These steps link Praça Cardos Câmara in Lapa with Rua Hermenegildo de Barros in Santa Teresa. Their official name is the Ladeira de Santa Teresa but

Arcos da Lapa

Escadaria Selarón

locals refer to them as the Escadaria Selarón – in homage to the Chilean artist who decorated them with colored and mirrored mosaic tiles. Although the bottom steps are safe in day time, taking the full walk along the steps is not advised. ◎ *Map W5 • Praça Cardos Câmara, Lapa*

Circo Voador

This concert arena and its coterie of musicians and artists have revitalized Lapa, which was once dangerous and decrepit. Shows at the Circo attracted visitors and brought new life to old *samba* clubs, encouraging new clubs to open. Some of Rio's best acts, including Seu Jorge, began here. The Circo is a great place to check out Rio's cutting-edge live talent. ◎ *Map W4 • Rua dos Arcos s/n, Lapa • (021) 2533 0354 • www.circovoador.com.br*

Feira do Rio Antigo

On the first Saturday of each month there is a lively antiques and bric-a-brac fair on Rua do Lavradio, northeast of Arcos da Lapa. The streets fill up with old-fashioned furniture and household items, as well as people dancing to live bands playing *samba* and, unusually for Rio, tango. ◎ *Map V4*

Two Nights of Music in Lapa

Friday

There is nowhere better to get acquainted with the bewildering diversity of Brazilian musical styles than in Lapa on a Friday night. Begin at around 8pm with an ice-cold *chopp* beer in **Belmonte Lapa** *(see p62)* on Avenida Mem de Sá (where there is a street party on Friday and Saturday nights). *Choro*, which was popular in Rio before *samba*, can be heard live at **Carioca da Gema** *(see p84)*, which is also on Avenida Mem da Sá. This club has a great pizza restaurant. At about 10pm, leave **Carioca da Gema** for some *gafieira* or ballroom *samba*, played by a big band fronted by a single singer. *Gafieira* is best heard some 300 ft (91 m) away at the **Clube dos Democraticos** *(see p84)*. Be prepared to dance and be danced with. After this, sample some live *samba* at the nearby **Casa de Mae Joana** or **Rio Scenarium** *(see p84)* – the former is small and intimate, the latter larger with a Bohemian atmosphere. Both play famous *samba* standards.

Saturday

If Friday has not left you exhausted, come back on Saturday evening to the **Circo Voador** for more Rio funk, or dance around Largo de Lapa to some northeastern Brazilian *forró* played on accordion, triangle, and *surdo* drum. Other options include *bossa nova* electronica at a venue such as **Espírito Santa** *(see p84)*, or more from the endless list of Brazilian musical styles *(see pp38–9)*.

Left **Carioca da Gema** Right **Clube dos Democráticos**

🔟 Bars and Clubs

1 Carioca da Gema
This is one of Rio's best *samba* and *choro* bars. Upstairs is a pizza restaurant, where different live acts play sets late into the night. ⊗ *Map W4 • Av Mem de Sá 79, Lapa • (021) 2221 0043*

2 Rio Scenarium
One of the larger *samba* clubs in Rio, this popular venue hosts live bands on the ground floor and has bars and dance floors on the upper levels. ⊗ *Map V3 • Rua do Lavradio 20, Lapa • (021) 3147 9000*

3 Sacrilégio
Excellent live acts play in this *samba* club, which is located in an 18th-century house decorated in green and white. ⊗ *Map V4 • Mem de Sá 81, Lapa • (021) 3970 1461*

4 Casa da Mãe Joana
One of Lapa's most traditional clubs is famous for its *samba* and *choro* bands. ⊗ *Map V4 • Av Gomes Freire 547, Lapa • (021) 2224 4071*

5 Espírito Santa
Upstairs is a restaurant decorated with modern art and a terrace that offers wonderful views of the city. Downstairs is a club that plays funk and Brazilian groove on Fridays. ⊗ *Map V6 • Rua Almirante Alexandrino 264, Santa Teresa • (021) 2507 4840*

6 Choperia Brazooka
Pounding with music from live rock bands, this huge venue has three bars over four floors and is a popular spot with loyal Lapa locals. ⊗ *Map W4 • Ave Mem de Sá 70, Lapa • (021) 2224 3236*

7 Teatro Odisséia
This converted three-storey warehouse rocks to the sound of live bands at weekends, and also puts on art exhibitions and plays. ⊗ *Map W4 • Av Mem de Sá 66, Lapa • (021) 2226 9691*

8 Armazém São Thiago
This quintessential Santa Teresa bar buzzes with charm and character, from the cabinet-lined walls to the loyal clientele. ⊗ *Map U6 • Rua Áurea 26, Santa Teresa • (021) 2232 0822*

9 Clube dos Democráticos
This 19th-century ballroom has a stage large enough for big *samba* bands with up to 20 members, and hosts ballroom *samba* and *gafieira* bands on weekends. ⊗ *Map V5 • Rua da Riachuelo 91, Lapa • (021) 2252 4611*

10 Circo Voador
The best of Rio's emerging funk acts play alongside established stars in Lapa's principal concert hall. Many well-known singers got their break here (see p83).

Price Categories

For a three-course
meal for one with half
a bottle of wine (or
equivalent meal), taxes,
and extra charges.

$ under US$15
$$ US$15–US$25
$$$ US$25–US$35
$$$$ US$35–US$50
$$$$$ over US$50

Left **Sobrenatural** Right **Bar do Arnaúdo's entrance**

Places to Eat

1 Bar do Mineiro

The tasty snacks here include *bolinhos de bacalhau* (salted cod fritters) and *feijoada* (bean and meat stew). ✎ *Map V6 • Rua Paschoal Carlos Magno 99 • (021) 2221 9227 • $*

2 Sobrenatural

Santa Teresa's most popular eatery serves excellent seafood. There is live *samba* and *choro* on Fridays. ✎ *Map V6 • Av Almirante Alexandrino 432, Santa Teresa • (021) 2224 1003 • $$$*

3 Aprazível

This open-air restaurant specializes in seafood and traditional Brazilian dishes like *galinhada caipira* (chicken risotto with *mineiro* sausage, chicory, and beans). ✎ *Map U6 • Rua Aprazível 62, Santa Teresa • (021) 2508 9174 • $$$$*

4 Adega do Pimenta

Enjoy the creative dishes on offer here, including roast rabbit with curried cauliflower. ✎ *Map V6 • Rua Almirante Alexandrino 296, Santa Teresa • (021) 2224 7554 • $$$*

5 Bar do Arnaúdo

This *boteco* serves *petiscos* and north-eastern mains, such as Bahian *moquecas* (fish stew) and *carne do sol* (salted beef). ✎ *Map U6 • Rua Almirante Alexandrino 316, Santa Teresa • (021) 2210 0817 • $$*

6 Alda Maria

This local bakery serves Portuguese cakes and pastries, including *pasteis de nata* (custard tarts). It has good coffee and a cozy atmosphere. ✎ *Map U6 • Rua Almirante Alexandrino, Santa Teresa • (021) 2232 1320 • $*

7 Mike's Haus

Feast on delicious *petiscos* and a range of German sausages, including Kalbsbratwurst and Nuernberger, at this popular restaurant. ✎ *Map V6 • Rua Almirante Alexandrino 1458A, Santa Teresa • (021) 2509 5248 • $$$*

8 Sansushi

Diners sit in small wooden booths in one of Rio's most traditional Japanese restaurants to eat sushi and noodles. ✎ *Map V6 • Rua Almirante Alexandrino 382, Santa Teresa • (021) 2252 0581 • $$$*

9 Térèze

The elegant restaurant in the Hotel Santa Teresa is pricey but highly rated. ✎ *Map U6 • Rua Felicia dos Santos, Santa Teresa • (021) 2221 1406 • $$$$$*

10 Goya Beira

A busy little *boteco* with a glass-fronted bar. Cariocas come here for a cold *chopp* (beer) and *petiscos* after work. ✎ *Map U5 • Largo das Neves 13, Santa Teresa • (021) 2232 5751 • $$*

Recommend your favorite restaurant on **traveldk.com**

Around Town – Santa Teresa and Lapa

85

Left **A juice bar on Copacabana** Right **Paintings at Vinícius, near Garota de Ipanema**

Copacabana, Ipanema, and Leblon

EVEN THOUGH MOST OF RIO DE JANEIRO CITY *lies away from the coast, its association with the beach remains strong, courtesy of the stunning Copacabana and Ipanema beaches, whose sweeping crescents of sand look south across the Atlantic Ocean. These beaches are backed by a series of bustling neighborhoods: Copacabana lies at the western end of Copacabana beach and Leme sits at its eastern extremity; Arpoador sits at Ipanema beach's eastern end, Leblon at its western end, and Ipanema lies in between. While Arpoador, Ipanema, and Leblon attract the exclusive beach crowd, vibrant Copacabana and Leme beaches are somewhat tawdry.*

Tourists at Copacabana beach

🔟 Sights

1. Praia de Copacabana
2. Ipanema and Leblon Beachlife
3. Ipanema's Fashionable Streets
4. Os Dois Irmãos
5. Garota de Ipanema
6. Juice Bars
7. Rua Dias Ferreira
8. Casa de Cultura Laura Alvim
9. Morro do Leme
10. Museu H. Stern

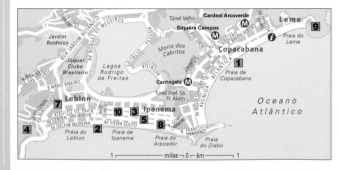

1 Praia de Copacabana

Rio's most famous stretch of beach is a vast 4-mile (6.4-km) sweep of powder-fine sand along the shores of the Atlantic. It is backed by a broad, four-lane avenue studded with towering hotels and Art Deco apartment blocks, the most famous being the Copacabana Palace hotel (see p112). The avenue is lined on either side by wave-patterned mosaic pavements and has cafés and juice kiosks running along its length (see pp24–5).

2 Ipanema and Leblon Beachlife

Ipanema and Leblon beaches are where fashion-conscious and gay and lesbian Rio comes to lounge and relax in the sun. An after-noon here is an essential Rio de Janeiro experience. Bring as little as possible. Sun-shades, deck chairs, snacks, and drinks are readily available on the beaches. If you plan on swimming, beware the strong waves and cold water (see pp26–7).

3 Ipanema's Fashionable Streets

Ruas Garcia d'Avila, Visconde de Pirajá, and Nascimento da Silva in Ipanema are home to the most exclusive designer boutiques, jewelry shops, and

Toulon in Ipanema

cafés in Rio (see pp90–91). Top Brazilian brands like Lenny, Andrea Saletto, and Antonio Bernardo vie for street space with international names such as Louis Vuitton. And although it is possible to find bargains in shops like Toulon (see p90), prices are generally well above the Brazilian average. ✎ Map M5 • Ipanema

4 Os Dois Irmãos

The "Two Brothers" – twin peaks that tower over Leblon – look particularly beautiful at dusk, when the sky turns pink and the waves are bottle-green. There is a look-out point from a gap in Os Dois Irmãos that boasts great views over Leblon and Ipanema, and is reachable from the beach end of Avenida Ataúlfo de Paiva in Leblon. ✎ Map K6 • Leblon

The Gay Pride flag on Ipanema beach

Morro do Leme

Garota de Ipanema

In the early 1960s, the poet Vinícius de Moraes and his composer friend Antônio Carlos Jobim met regularly in this little bar. Inspired by a beautiful girl who used to pass by, the duo wrote the song *Garota de Ipanema*. When Brazilian guitarist João Gilberto, his wife Astrud, and US jazz saxophonist Stan Getz recorded it in English as *The Girl from Ipanema*, they popularized *bossa nova*. ◎ *Map N5*
• *Rua Vinícius de Moraes 49, Ipanema*
• *(021) 2523 3787*

Juice Bars

The streets near the beaches at Ipanema and Copacabana are dotted with bars serving juices made from either freshly crushed fruit or frozen pulp. Cariocas usually begin their day with a glass of juice and a snack. Be sure to ask for *pouco açúcar* (just a little sugar), unless you have a very sweet tooth *(see p37)*.

Rua Dias Ferreira

Some of the best restaurants and bars in the city line this upmarket, chic street at the end of Leblon. It is worth heading down here for an evening stroll before deciding where to dine. Restaurants range from family-run businesses, such as Celeiro *(see p91)*, to the likes of Zuka *(see p44)* and Sushi Leblon *(see p91)*, which were founded by chefs who previously worked in New York or London. Cuisines range from French to modern Brazilian, Japanese, *churrascaria* *(see p110)*, and Asian-South American fusion. Dress codes are informal. ◎ *Map K5*

An exhibit at Casa de Cultura Laura Alvim

Bossa Nova

Bossa nova is gentrified *samba*, sung in a spoken or whispered voice *(see pp38–9)*. Born in the 1950s, when Moraes, Jobim, and Gilberto began composing songs together, *bossa nova* became internationally famous with Camus' 1960 film "Black Orpheus". It can be heard at Toca do Vinícius *(see p55)* on Sunday afternoons.

Casa de Cultura Laura Alvim

Patron of the arts Laura Agostini Alvim founded this arts center in her old house in Ipanema. It exhibits artworks from Alvim's

The Lagoa and Jardim Botânico are only a 10-minute bus or taxi ride from Ipanema or Copacabana.

friends and admirers, including Angelo de Aquino, Paulo Roberto Leal, Roberto Moriconi, and Rubens Guerchman, and hosts visiting exhibitions, small concerts, and book launches. It also has an arts cinema and theater. Plays are mostly in Portuguese. ❧ *Map P6 • Av Vieira Souto 176, Ipanema • (021) 2332 2016 • Open 3–9pm Tue–Sun*

Morro do Leme
This boulder hill watches over Copacabana from the Leme end of the beach. It is a great spot to visit on a Sunday afternoon, when live *samba* bands play near the seafood kiosks. Paths and a climbing trail wind around the rock, but these are not safe without a guide – assaults and robberies are not uncommon here *(see p25)*.

Museu H. Stern
The workshops in Brazil's largest jewelry chain are open to tour groups, who can watch stones being cut, polished, and set. The guides are knowledge-able about these processes, so be sure to ask questions. Visits finish at the museum shop, where a series of carefully lit display cases show pieces from H. Stern's latest jewelry catalogue. ❧ *Map M5 • Rua Garcia d'Avila 133, Ipanema • (021) 2106 0000*

Jewelry at Museu H. Stern

A Day at the Beach

Morning

🕐 Pack your beach bag with the minimum and bring a moderate amount of cash. To blend in with the locals, women should slip on a *tanga* (bikini) and a *canga* (sarong). Men should dress in board shorts over a *sunga* (rectangular-cut speedos), and wear a loose T-shirt. Finish the look with sunglasses and *chinelos* (flip-flops) – all available in shops at Ipanema and Copacabana. Put a novel and sun cream (factor 30) in your beach bag and head to one of the many juice kiosks in Ipanema and Copacabana for a coconut milk or an *açai (see p37)*. Arrive on the beach before 9:30am to sunbathe. You will not overheat as the water here is surprisingly chilly. Swim at Leblon, which has the cleanest water. Areas with strong currents are always flagged.

Afternoon

Beachwear is acceptable everywhere except in formal lunchtime restau-rants. Have a relaxed meal, a coffee, and browse in the shops along **Rua Garcia d'Avila**. From 3:30pm people begin surfing, cycling, and playing beach volleyball or soccer. Mingle with the locals or just jog along the warm sand. Romantic strolls along the waterfront are wonderful in the afternoon and beach massages are popular as the air gets cool. After sunset, head to a *boteco* like **Garota de Ipanema** in Ipanema for an ice-cold beer. Return to the hotel to change before going out to one of the restaurants on **Rua Dias Ferrela**.

Left **Busy Feira Hippie Market** Right **Clothes at Toulon**

Shopping

Feira Hippie Market
Praça General Osório's Sunday bric-a-brac market has stalls selling crafts, household items, and clothing. ◉ Map P5
• Praça General Osório • Open 7am–7pm

Shopping Rio Design Leblon
This mall on Leblon's largest shopping street has more than 70 shops and a little cinema. It also hosts concerts. ◉ Map L5 • Av Ataulfo de Paiva 270 • (021) 3206 9100

Raiz Forte Produtos da Terra
Herbal medicines and natural products like *guaraná* powder and *açaí* pulp *(see p37)* can be found here. ◉ Map L5 • Av Ataulfo de Paiva 1160, Leblon • (021) 2259 0744

Toca do Vinícius
Choro, *samba*, and *bossa nova* music fill the shelves of this shop. You can listen to CDs before deciding what to buy.
◉ Map N5 • Rua Vinícius de Moraes 129, Ipanema • (021) 2247 5227

Toulon
Head to Toulon to stock up on jeans, jackets, shirts and swimwear. ◉ Map M5 • Rua Visconde de Pirajá 540, Ipanema • (021) 2239 2195

Andrea Saletto
This fashionable Brazilian women's label sells clothes made from high-quality fabrics. ◉ Map M5 • Rua Nascimento Silva 244, Ipanema • (021) 2522 5858

Baratas do Ribeiro
A shrine for *Carioca* music lovers, this shop stocks more than 15,000 CDs and thousands of second-hand books, many in English. ◉ Map R3 • Rua Barata Ribeiro 354, Copacabana • (021) 2256 8634

Gilson Martins
This shop's range of bright, funky bags are crafted from materials such as leather, plastic, and vinyl, and come in a variety of Carioca shapes – from a soccer ball to the Sugar Loaf.
◉ Map N5 • Rua Visconde de Pirajá 462B, Ipanema • (021) 2227 6178

Victor Hugo
Brazil's counterpart to Louis Vuitton, Victor Hugo attracts Rio's sophisticated set with its collection of branded wallets, purses, handbags, and personal luggage. ◉ Map N5 • Rua Visconde de Pirajá 507, Ipanema • (021) 2259 9699

Maria Bonita
Known for her tops and famous jersey dresses with wrap fronts and high elasticated waists, Maria Bonita is popular internationally. ◉ Map N5
• Rua Vinícius de Moraes 149, Ipanema
• (021) 2523 4093

Alessandro e Frederico Café

TOP10 Places to Eat

1 Forneria São Sebastião
This Italian restaurant specializes in pizzas and gourmet burgers in *panini* rolls. ◈ *Map M5 • Rua Aníbal de Mendonça 112, Ipanema • (021) 2540 8045 • $$$*

2 Sushi Leblon
Rio's most celebrated Japanese restaurant was the first in the city to experiment with Japanese-Western fusion cuisine. ◈ *Map K5 • Rua Dias Ferreira 256, Leblon • (021) 2274 1342 • $$$$*

3 Alessandro e Frederico Café
A favorite with Ipanema's socialites, this restaurant serves tasty salmon in sweet and sour sauce and excellent coffee. ◈ *Map M5 • Rua Garcia d'Avila 134D, Ipanema • (021) 2521 0828 • $$$*

4 Zazá Bistrô Tropical
This brightly colored bistro, a block from the beach, serves Mediterranean and Eastern food, including Vietnamese rolls. ◈ *Map N6 • Rua Joana Angélica 40, Ipanema • (021) 2247 9101 • $$$$*

5 Celeiro
Celeiro serves a broad range of delicious organic salads and light meals, as well as cakes and juices. ◈ *Map K5 • Rua Dias Ferreira 199, Leblon • (021) 2274 7843 • $$$*

6 Fellini
One of the best buffet restaurants in Leblon, Fellini serves meat, poultry, and fish dishes, generous salads, and good vegetarian dishes. ◈ *Map L5 • Rua Gen Urquiza 104, Leblon • (021) 2511 3600 • $$$*

7 Casa da Feijoada
Enjoy a traditional Sunday lunch of the national dish *feijoada*, which is made from black beans, pork, and beef off-cuts. ◈ *Map P6 • Rua Prudente de Morais 10, Ipanema • (021) 2247 2776 • $$$*

8 New Natural
This vegetarian and whole foods restaurant offers salads, soups, and soya meat casseroles. ◈ *Map N5 • Rua Barão da Torre 173, Ipanema • (021) 2247 9363 • $$*

9 Le Pré Catalan
Head here for tasty Franco-Brazilian cuisine. The set menu in particular is of excellent value. ◈ *Map Q5 • Sofitel, Av Atlântica 4240, Copacabana • (021) 2525 1232 • $$$$$*

10 Cipriani
The Copacabana Palace's *(see p112)* haute cuisine restaurant is related to the Cipriani in New York and Venice and features excellent north Italian dishes. ◈ *Map R3 • Av Atlântica 1702, Copacabana • (021) 2545 8747 • $$$$$*

For other restaurants in this area **See pp44–5.**

The beach at Cabo Frio

Rio de Janeiro State

RIO DE JANEIRO STATE *is one of Brazil's most beautiful regions. Its coastline is dotted with resorts and pretty colonial fishing towns, and fringed with glorious white-sand beaches. The mountainous interior features the former summer retreats of Brazil's Portuguese royal family, who struggled to adjust to the heat of urban Rio. Many of the higher slopes remain covered by the Mata Atlântica, or the Atlantic coastal rain forest, which preserves Brazil's most diverse ecosystem. Much of the forest is protected by a series of national and state parks, including Itatiaia and the Serra dos Órgãos, both of which offer superb bird-watching and wildlife-spotting opportunities.*

Serra dos Órgãos

Sights

1 Mata Atlântica
2 Búzios
3 Serra dos Órgãos
4 Petrópolis
5 Teresópolis
6 Parque National do Itatiaia
7 Região dos Lagos
8 Cabo Frio
9 Paraty
10 Ilha Grande

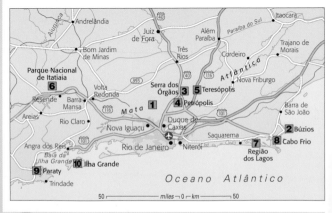

Previous pages **A colorful Carnaval parade**

Mata Atlântica

Brazil's Atlantic coastal rain forest – the largest section of which lies in the states of Rio de Janeiro, São Paulo, and Paraná – is home to some 20,000 plant species, 950 bird species, and more than 20 endemic threatened mammals, including jaguars and pumas. The rain forest is home to a lush array of orchids and abundant wildlife. Ecotourism has started to play an increasingly important role in the conservation of the forest.
◈ Map B2

Búzios

When actress Brigitte Bardot first visited it, this bustling resort town was a quiet fishing hamlet on a chaparral-covered peninsula fringed with pristine beaches. Búzios still feels low-key compared to resorts in the Mediterranean or Mexico, but all the beaches are now backed with hotels, and the fishing village has grown into a small town whose cobbled streets are lined with chic boutiques and upscale restaurants. ◈ Map C2
• www.buziosonline.com.br

Statue of Brigitte Bardot in Búzios

Serra dos Órgãos

This mountain range to the northeast of Rio city got its name from a series of bizarre rock stacks shaped like organ pipes. Climbing, trekking, and bird-watching here are superb. ◈ Map B2
• www.riohiking.com

Petrópolis

Emperor Dom Pedro II's summer retreat, Petrópolis was founded in the Serra dos Órgãos in 1843 and was connected to Rio city by train. Much of the town was designed by the German architect Julius Friedrich Köler and settled by wealthy Cariocas. It is replete with mansions and palaces, including the Museu Imperial, the former home of the royal family.
◈ Map B2 • Museu Imperial: Rua da Imperatriz 220, Petrópolis; (024) 2245 5550; open 11am–5:30pm Tue–Sun

Museu Imperial, Petrópolis

Biodiversity

The Mata Atlântica, or Atlantic coastal rain forest, is isolated from other major rain forest blocks in South America by the continent's arid interior, and thus has a diverse and unique mix of plant and animal types, many of which exist only here. Today, less than 8 percent of the original forest remains and Brazilians are realizing that ecotourism is crucial to the Mata Atlântica's survival.

Teresópolis

This rather scruffy mountain town, which lies 57 miles (91 km) northeast of Rio city, was the favorite summer retreat of Teresa Cristina Maria de Bourbon-Sicílias e Bragança, the empress consort of Dom Pedro II. The town, which is the highest in Rio de Janeiro state and the closest to the Serra dos Órgãos, is the summer training camp for the Brazilian football team. It comes alive on weekends with a bustling artisan fair. ◈ *Map B2*

Parque Nacional do Itatiaia

Brazil's oldest national park is the best place in the state for seeing neotropical wildlife and is also one of the country's best bird-watching spots. Itatiaia boasts wonderful views out over the mountains and treetops, all the way to the coast. There are various hotels located within the park; many have trails that lead directly into the forest, making them popular with families.
◈ *Map A2* • *Estrada Parque Nacional Km 8.5, Itatiaia* • *(024) 3352 1292* • *Adm*
• *www.ibama.gov.br/parna_itatiaia*

Região dos Lagos

The picturesque coastal landscape between Rio de Janeiro and Búzios is fringed with miles of white, talcum-fine sandy beaches that are pounded by powerful surf. The hinterland is broken by a series of brackish lakes that give the region its name – Região dos Lagos, or the Lake District. Resort towns including Cabo Frio, Arraial do Cabo, and Saquarema are all good bases for visitors who are interested in exploring the area. All are easily reachable by bus or car from the city in less than three hours. ◈ *Map C2*
• *www.riolagos.com.br*

Cabo Frio

The largest resort town in the Região dos Lagos is a very popular weekend escape

An Ilha Grande seashore

with Cariocas and people from the neighboring state of Minas Gerais, who come for the beaches, surfing, snorkeling, and scuba diving just to the south of the town. Although Cabo Frio has rather uninspiring architecture, it is packed with numerous hotels, shops, and restaurants. ◈ *Map C2*

Boats moored at Paraty quay

9 Paraty
This colonial town situated 152 miles (245 km) southwest of Rio city grew rich on gold that was transported along the Caminho do Ouro trail from neighboring Minas Gerais in the 18th century. The historic center, which was declared a UNESCO World Heritage Site in 1958, is filled with streets of white-washed Portuguese houses and Baroque churches. There are also many beaches nearby. ◈ *Map A3*

10 Ilha Grande
There are no roads on this forested island just south of Rio city, and facilities are limited. How-ever, the beaches and trekking are breathtaking. Ferries and chartered fishing boats leave for the island's capital, Abraão, from the port town of Angra dos Reis, which is well-connected to Rio de Janeiro by a bus service. ◈ *Map A2*

Rio de Janeiro State

A Day in Paraty

Morning
🕐 Stay in the historical center and after an early start, walk down to the long quay. The sun rising behind the forest-covered hills of the **Mata Altântica** is a magnificent sight.

☕ Have breakfast in one of the little cafés near the quay before chartering a boat for a half-day cruise around the bay. This will include a snorkeling stop at one of the small islands nearby, as well as visits to beaches. Request a lunch stop at the popular **Oatimbaú** *(see p99)* restaurant, which is run by a local fisherman on one tiny island.

Afternoon
Explore the town in the early afternoon. Maps are available from the tourist office at the gateway to the historic center. It is hard to get lost as the center is only five streets deep and eight wide. All the sights can be visited in three or four hours. There are several Baroque churches, the most interesting of which is the **Nossa Senhora do Rosário e São Benedito**, the church of the African slaves, which is on Rua do Comércio. It is plain but has a special atmosphere. It is also worth visiting the town's museum, which focuses on the gold rush.

Evening
In the evening, dine in one of the town's many excellent restaurants. Follow it with a night out at the adult puppet theater in the **Teatro Espaço** on Rua Dona Geralda, whose touching, tragi-comic shows have toured Europe and the USA.

Every winter Paraty hosts the Festa Literária Internacional de Paraty (see p32), an internationally renowned literary festival.

Left **The Serra dos Órgãos** Right **The Bay of Paraty**

🔟 Activities in Rio State

1 Bird-watching in the Mata Atlântica

The Atlantic coastal rain forest is one of the top bird-watching destinations in the world. The Tucanos lodge located here has good guides and facilities. ◈ *Map C2 • Tucanos Lodge: Caixa Postal 98125, Cachoeiras de Macacu; (021) 2649 1557; www.serradostucanos.com.br*

2 Hiking in the Serra dos Órgãos

This mountain range offers hiking, rock climbing, and a chance to spot rare mammals and birds. Hiking is safest with a tour company. ◈ *Map B2 • www.riohiking.com.br*

3 Hiking in Itatiaia

Brazil's first national park is set in scenic mountains *(see p96)* and offers great hiking routes. Walks can take a day or more. Tour companies can organize guides *(see p102)*.

4 Diving in Cabo Frio

The best diving in southeast Brazil is around Cabo Frio and Arraial do Cabo. Turtles are a common sight and brightly colored dolphin fish can also be seen. ◈ *Map C2 • www.cabofriosub.com.br*

5 Cruising the Bay of Paraty

Most cruises that leave from Paraty take half a day. Charter a boat through a boat operator such as Tuca or a tour company such as Angatu, and visit the bay's many beaches. ◈ *Map A2 • Tuca: (024) 9948 0529 • Angatu: www.angatu.com*

6 Wildlife in Regua

The rare woolly spider-monkey is found in the Reserva Ecológica de Guapi Assu (Regua) preserve. The bird-watching here is great. ◈ *Map C2 • Regua: Caixa Postal 98112, Cachoeiras de Macacu; (021) 9859 2080; www.regua.co.uk*

7 A Tour of the Royal Cities and Coffee Towns

Petrópolis, Teresópolis, and Vassouras are accessible by car from Rio in a day, but it is preferable to spread your trip over a few days. Rosa Thompson runs the best tours. ◈ *www.rozbrazil.com*

8 Luxury Stays in Paraty

Rent private villas in the colonial center and on the surrounding islands. These usually come with a boat and chef and are popular during the town's International Literary Festival *(see p33).*

9 A Weekend in Petrópolis

The Locanda della Mimosa is a fine-dining restaurant and a luxury boutique hotel with six rooms. Gourmet weekends are organized with special rates for groups. ◈ *Map B2 • Alameda das Mimosas 30, Vale Florido, near Petrópolis • (024) 2233 5405 • www.locanda.com.br*

10 A Spa Break in Paraty

Bromelias Spa offers packages that include *reiki,* massage, and other treatments. This can be combined with other tours in Paraty, which is just 30 minutes away *(see p117).*

The interior of Merlin O Mago

Price Categories

For a three-course meal for one with half a bottle of wine (or equivalent meal), taxes, and extra charges.

$	under US$15
$$	US$15–US$25
$$$	US$25–US$35
$$$$	US$35–US$50
$$$$$	over US$50

ᵀᴼᴾ10 Places to Eat

Satyricon
Rio's most popular seafood restaurant began with this branch in Búzios. The dining room overlooks the Atlantic and is great for a romantic meal. ◎ Map C2 • Av Jose Bento Ribeiro Dantas, Orla Bardot 500, Búzios • (022) 2623 1595 • $$$$

Cigalon
This mock-French bistro serves decent classics. The seafood is great, the wine list commendable, and the ambience intimate. ◎ Map C2 • Rua das Pedras 199, Búzios • (022) 2623 0932 • $$$

Merlin O Mago
A Cordon Bleu-trained German chef owns this intimate, candlelit restaurant. The endlessly inventive menu and excellent wine list are a labor of love. ◎ Map A2 • Rua do Comércio 376, Paraty • (024) 3371 2157 • $$$

Bartholomeu
Paraty's best steaks are brought in from Argentina and cooked to perfection here. Come at sunset for cocktails at the little bar. The *caipirinhas* are superb. ◎ Map A2 • Rua Dr Samuel Costa 176, Paraty • (024) 3371 5032 • $$$

Punta Di Vino
Paraty's best pizzeria is also its finest seafood restaurant. The wine, live music, and general atmosphere are first class ◎ Map A2 • Rua da Matriz 129, Paraty • (024) 3371 1348 • $$$

Catimbaú
With a delightful setting on the edge of an island in an emerald-green sea, Catimbaú is only accessible by boat from Paraty. The menu is limited to supremely fresh fish. ◎ Map A2 • Baía de Paraty • (024) 3371 1847 • $$$

Le Gite D'Indaiatiba
This French-Brazilian fusion restaurant located on a forest-covered hill is very popular. ◎ Map A2 • Rodovia Rio-Santos (BR–101) Km 558, Graúna, Paraty • (024) 3371 7174 • $$$$ • www.legitedindaiatiba.com.br

Villa Verde
Italian dishes and seafood are served at this restaurant and bar, which is situated in a flower-filled garden 4 miles (7 km) from the town center. ◎ Map A2 • Rodovia Paraty Cunha, Km 6.5, Paraty • (024) 3371 7808 • $$ • www.villaverdeparaty.com.br

Thai Paraty
Some of the most authentic Thai food in South America is created in this brightly colored restaurant in Paraty. The green curry is excellent. ◎ Map A2 • Rua Noel Rosa 9, Portal das Artes, Paraty • (024) 3371 2170 • $$$

Locanda della Mimosa
The menu at this eatery, set in a beautiful colonial house, is heavy on game, and the wine list boasts around 3,000 wines. ◎ Map B2 • Alameda das Mimosas 30, Vale Florido, near Petrópolis • (024) 2233 5405 • $$$$ • www.locanda.com.br

"Km" in an address indicates the exit to take. "BR–101" refers to Brazil's second major highway.

STREETSMART

Planning Your Visit
102

Getting There
and Around
103

General Information
104

Banking and
Communications
105

Gay and Lesbian Rio
106

Budget Tips
107

Health and Security
108

Things to Avoid
109

Dining Tips
110

Accommodation Tips
111

Places to Stay
112

RIO DE JANEIRO'S TOP 10

Left **Estádio do Maracanã** Right **Pharmacy goods**

Planning Your Visit

1 When to Go
Rio is beautiful at any time of the year. It is wet and warm from November to February, and dry and sunny during the rest of the year. Popular times to visit are December and during Carnaval, which usually falls in February or March.

2 What to Bring
Bring clothing for temperatures that can range from 95°F (35°C) to 59°F (15°C). A sweater is necessary when visiting national parks, where a mosquito net could also prove useful. Items such as sunscreen, insect repellent, and beach wear can all be bought during your stay.

3 What to Wear
Rio is a very informal city and gives you the opportunity to dress down. *Chinelos* (flip-flops) or sandals are commonly worn in the beach neighborhoods while light walking shoes are good for the city center and for forest walks. Try to avoid ostentatious outfits and leave costly watches and jewelry at home.

4 Consulates and Embassies
Many countries have Brazilian embassies and consulates with websites offering advice on planning your trip to Rio, including organizing visas and staying safe.

5 Visas
EU citizens do not require visas for Brazil. Visitors from the USA, Canada, Australia, and New Zealand do. Visas are mandatory for any visitor who plans to stay in the country for longer than 180 days or plans to work in Brazil.

6 Tour Operators
A great way to see the attractions in Rio de Janeiro is on a tour. They prove to be the most practical option for a range of attractions, from soccer matches at Maracanã *(see p42)* to cruises in Guanabara Bay. Tours to various national parks are also available.

7 Learning Portuguese
Portuguese is a difficult but melodic language. Although speakers of Spanish will find that many of the words look familiar, pronunciation is radically different. It is important to bring a dictionary and a phrase book as few locals speak any other languages.

8 Customs
There is no duty on up to US$500 in cash or the equivalent value in personal items. If you plan on transferring residence to Brazil, you can bring in your belongings duty free if authorized by the Brazilian Embassy in your home country.

9 Health and Vaccines
Visitors to Brazil can be asked to provide a yellow fever vaccination certificate upon entering the country. It is also a good idea to have vaccines for tetanus, polio, and hepatitis A. Dengue fever, which is transmitted by mosquitoes, is present in Rio, but there is no vaccine for this *(see p109)*. Private health care, dental treatment, and pharmacies are at the same standards as Europe and the USA.

10 Background Reading
Good places to start are Joseph Page's *The Brazilians* and Alex Bellos's *Futebol – The Brazilian Way of Life*, which tells the story of soccer in Brazil.

Tours

Birding & Wildlife Tours
• www.regua.co.uk

Diving • www. cabofriosub.com.br

Driving Tours • www. privatetours.com.br

Guanabara Bay
• www.saveiros.com.br

Helicopter Tours
• www.helisight.com.br

Hiking
• www.riohiking.com.br

Walks in Rio city
• www.culturalrio. com.br

Previous pages **A *favela* painting in a Rio market**

Left **Aircraft at Aeroporto Santos Dumont** Right **Local taxi**

🔟 Getting There and Around

1 Aeroporto Internacional Antônio Carlos Jobim

Rio's international airport, which lies 9 miles (15 km) north of the city center, is often referred to by its former name – Galeão. It also handles some domestic flights. Allow at least 1 hour to get there during rush hour. There is a Riotur information center, 24-hour ATMs, and a currency exchange on the premises, as well as taxis and shuttle buses to the center and the domestic airport, Santos Dumont. ✪ Map B5
• www.infraero.gov.br

2 Aeroporto Santos Dumont

Rio's domestic airport lies half a mile (1 km) south of the city center. It offers shuttle flights to São Paulo and onward connections to many of Brazil's other state capitals and major cities. Taxis to Ipanema and Copacabana are around US$15 from here. Buy a ticket at the taxi booths inside the terminal. ✪ Map J2
• www.infraero.gov.br

3 Airport Buses

The best airport buses are the Real Auto air-conditioned coaches, which leave from terminals 1 and 2 at Aeroporto Antônio Carlos Jobim and connect to the city center bus station, Aeroporto Santos Dumont, Glória, Flamengo, Botafogo,

Copacabana, Ipanema, Gávea, São Conrado, and Barra da Tijuca. ✪ (021) 3035 6700 • Departure every 30 minutes between 5:30am and 11:30pm • www.realautoonibus.com.br

4 City Buses

Buses running through Rio are usually clearly labeled with their destination on the front. They should be avoided at night, however, when petty theft is common. ✪ www.rioonibus.com

5 Inter-City Buses

International and interstate buses leave from the Rodoviária Novo Rio. The station has a Riotur information booth (for hotel bookings), left luggage, ATMs, money exchanges, shops, and cafés. Taxis to Ipanema and Copacabana cost around US$10. Be careful at the bus station, which attracts thieves. ✪ Map F1 • Av Francisco Bicalho 1 • (021) 3213 1800 • www. novorio.com.br

6 Taxis

Yellow and blue taxis are common around Rio. While not all of them are registered, those that are operate from hotels or the taxi stands in each neighborhood.

7 Metro

The best means of transport in the city, Rio's subway runs from the north to Ipanema through the city center.

It is safe, clean, reliable, and cheap. Taking cabs from Ipanema, Leblon, or other outlying areas to the nearest metro station is worthwhile. ✪ 5am–midnight Mon–Sat, 7am–11pm Sun & hols, 24 hrs during Carnaval week
• www.metrorio.com.br

8 Car Rental and Driving

Renting a car is costly and it is worth organizing a deal before leaving for Brazil. Most major car rentals are represented in the city and have offices at the airports. Driving within the city is confusing as there are many one-way systems and parking is difficult. It is best to use public transport within the city itself and hire a car for Rio state. It is wise to avoid driving after dark.

9 Private Drivers

Hotels and tour companies can organize private drivers. It is an expensive option – you can expect to pay around US$100 for a full day.

10 Ferries

Ferries traverse Guanabara Bay and the busiest crossing is between Praça XV in Rio's city center and Niterói. Taking 20 minutes for a ferry ride and under 5 for a catamaran, boats are a quicker and far cheaper option than cabs. Ferries leave every 10 minutes.

 Free metro maps are available at most ticket booths in the metro system.

Left **Walking on the streets of Rio** Center **Shopping mall** Right **Local newspaper**

General Information

1 Disabled Travelers

While disabled facilities are poor in Brazil, they can be found in airports, bus stations, malls, and some hotels in Rio. The Society for Accessible Travel and Hospitality (SATH) offers useful tips on its website. ✪ www.sath.org

2 Tourist Offices

There are tourist booths in the airports and bus stations, and main offices in Copacabana, Ipanema, and the city center. Embratur and Riotur have useful websites (guiaoficial.com.br, turismo.gov.br) in Portuguese and English.
✪ Rio Convention and Visitors' Bureau: Map Q1
• Rua Guilhermina Guinle 272 • (021) 2266 9750
• 9am–5pm Mon–Fri
• www.rcvb.com.br

3 Women Travelers

Rio is a welcoming city and women are generally treated courteously. To ward off unwanted advances, firmly say me deixa em paz, por favor (leave me alone, please). Make sure you use taxis only from taxi points or hotels.

4 Opening Hours

Banks are open on weekdays from 9 or 10am until 3 or 4pm, but currency exchanges often open an hour later. Post office timings vary but they are usually open from 8am to 5pm. Shops are open from 9am until 6pm from Monday to Saturday, and malls stay open in the week from 10am until 10 or 11pm, and later on Saturdays.

5 Walking

During the day, the city center and beach neighborhoods of Ipanema, Leblon, and Copacabana can be explored on foot, while longer distances are best covered by taxi or metro. Use taxis when out at night for safety reasons.

6 SESC Cultural Centers

Rio de Janeiro is replete with cultural centers. These include SESCs, which are found in neighborhoods all over the city. These centers show some of the most interesting local musical acts as well as theater, art, and cinema. Most SESCs have restaurants.
✪ www.sescrj.com.br

7 Newspapers and Magazines

The principal papers and news magazines are O Globo, A Folha de São Paulo, Veja, Istoé, and Época. They are establishment-owned and right wing. Veja, which comes out on Fridays, has a useful arts section with listings for music shows and other events. The Rio Times, a free monthly English newspaper, is distributed to hotels, restaurants, and other outlets.

8 Websites

Together with the Rio de Janeiro tourist office (Riotur) and Embratur websites, www.brazilmax.com and www.ipanema.com are useful English-language websites for information about the city.

9 Traveling with Children

Children are very much a part of all aspects of life in Brazil and are almost always welcome – even in bars, botecos, and the most exclusive restaurants. They are generally greeted by Cariocas with great enthusiasm and affection.

10 Electricity

Electricity in Rio comes in both 200 volts and 110 volts. Most houses and even hotel rooms have both.

Public Holidays

New Year's Day or Reveillon (Jan 1); Carnaval (Week of Ash Wednesday, Feb/Mar); Good Friday and Easter (Mar/Apr); Tiradentes Day (Apr 21); Labor Day (May 1); Corpus Christi (62 days after Good Friday); Independence Day (Sep 7); Children's Day (Oct 12); All Souls' Day (Nov 2); Proclamation of the Republic Day (Nov 15); Christmas Day (Dec 25)

For general information about traveling to Brazil visit www.braziltourism.org

Left **Branch of Banco do Brasil** Center **A post box** Right **Telephone booth**

²⁰⁄₁₀ Banking and Communications

1 Currency
The Brazilian currency, the *real* (R$, plural *reais*), is divided into 100 *centavos*. The largest note is R$100. Small shops struggle to change R$100, R$50, and R$20 notes, making R$10 and R$5 the most commonly used notes. R$1 notes are being phased out in favor of coins.

2 Credit Cards
American Express, Visa, MasterCard, Diners Club, and other major international credit cards are accepted at most places. Credit cards can be used to withdraw money from ATMs throughout Rio. They should not be taken to the beach, where petty theft is common.

3 Traveler's Checks
Traveler's checks are next to useless in Brazil, where surcharges and taxes for their usage are prohibitively high in the few banks that accept them. It is more convenient to use a credit card for major expenses, such as hotel bills.

4 ATMs
Automatic Teller Machines, or *caixas electronicas*, found throughout Rio, are the easiest way to get cash. Withdrawals are limited to between R$600 and R$1,000 per transaction and two transactions per day. For safety reasons,

ATMs stop functioning after 10pm, some as early as 8pm. Always try to use them during the day.

5 Cash
Bring notes in various denominations so that you have *reais* on arrival. Euros and US dollars are the most widely accepted foreign currencies for exchange in Rio, and US dollars are also accepted by large hotels. Major banks change money, but the exchange rates are sometimes poorer than those at *casas de câmbio* (exchange offices).

6 Cell Phones
Cell phone services in Brazil are antiquated. Many international networks do not have arrangements with national services. Visitors can buy a SIM card on arrival, although registration is complex. Dialing charges can be high and users pay extraordinarily expensive rates when receiving calls from outside Rio state.

7 Public Telephones
Public telephones, known as *orelhões* (big ears) because of their unusual shape, are common in Rio. They accept *cartões telefônicos* (phone cards), available at newsstands and post offices, but no coins. For long-distance calls, dial the three- or four-digit code of a *prestadora* (service

provider) before the area or country code, which drops the zero. You can use any provider, but it is cheapest to use the code displayed in the call box.

8 Internet Cafés
There are plenty of Internet cafés in Rio, especially in Botafogo, Copacabana, Ipanema, and Leblon. Most hotels have Internet access, and some even offer wireless broadband in rooms.

9 Television
Brazil's TV Globo is one of the largest television producers in the world and is famous for its soaps. The plot of the evening soap is a popular Carioca conversation piece. Most hotels in Rio only show Brazilian television. Some of the more expensive hotels offer satellite TV, which has European channels, CNN, and BBC World News.

10 Post Offices
Correios (post offices) are widespread and can be identified by a yellow and blue sign. Postcards are cheap but the system of pricing for letters and parcels sent to Europe or the USA is complex and prices vary greatly from office to office and clerk to clerk. Express deliveries are known as SEDEX. Most post offices operate from 9am to 5pm Monday to Friday, from 10am to 1pm on Saturdays, and are closed on Sundays.

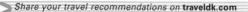

Left **Gay Pride Parade** Right **Gay flag at Ipanema beach**

🔟 Gay and Lesbian Rio

1 Acceptance
Rio may seem liberal and open-minded but, like the rest of Brazil, it is conservative at heart. Homophobic jokes are considered acceptable by many Cariocas. Attitudes to gay men and women in Copacabana and Ipanema are far more enlightened than they are in the city center or in the rest of Rio state.

2 On the Beach
The Farme Gay beach, a stretch of Ipanema beach between Postos 8 and 9, is the favorite daytime meeting place for Rio's gay and lesbian community. Look for the rainbow flag, which is displayed with pride by beach vendors in the area. Party promoters often distribute flyers here. 🅂 Map N6

3 On the Street
Rua Teixeira de Melo and its adjacent streets are the hub for gays and lesbians in Ipanema come early evening. You'll find an eclectic crowd here, circulating between cafés and clubs like Galeria and Dama de Ferro. 🅂 Galeria Café: Map P5; Rua Teixeira de Melo 31; (021) 2523 3250 • Dama de Ferro: Map N5 Rua Vinícius de Moraes 288; (021) 2247 2330

4 Nightlife
There are plenty of gay-friendly clubs and bars in Rio – especially around Ipanema and Copacabana beaches. The 00 (see p47) club attracts a sophisticated party crowd and The Week nightclub is always packed. 🅂 00 (Zero Zero): Map L4; Av Padre Leonel Franca 240, Gávea; (021) 2540 8041 • The Week: Map K4; Rua Sacadura Cabral 154; (021) 2253 1020

5 Le Boy Carnaval Ball
The popular Le Boy disco hosts a colorful gay ball during Carnaval. The venue is known for its pounding mix of samba and club music and dance shows from go-go boys. 🅂 Map Q6 • Rua Raul Pompeia 102, Copacabana • (021) 2513 4993 • Adm • www.leboy. com.br

6 Gay Pride Parade
The mid-October Gay Pride Parade attracts as many as a million visitors to Rio. It starts at lunchtime on Copacabana and moves along the beach, spilling over into neighboring Ipanema and Leblon and finishing up in Leme. There are many accompanying events. 🅂 www.gaypridebrazil.org

7 Banda de Ipanema
This parade is one of the best blocos of Carnaval (see p40). It attracts a wonderfully mixed crowd, from drag queens, transsexuals, and general gay revelers to straight couples and families with kids. The parade takes place on Carnaval Saturday and Tuesday. 🅂 Map P5 • Praça General Osório, Ipanema

8 Drag Queens
The city has long had its own unique cross-dressing scene, which draws on imagery from uniquely Carioca gay icons, like Carmen Miranda. It comes to the fore at Carnaval time with florid costumes and enormous head-dresses. One of Rio's most famous historical celebrities, João Francisco dos Santos, or "Madame Satã", was a drag queen in the 1920s.

9 Gala Gay
This wonderfully colorful, over-the-top Carnaval ball is the biggest event on the Rio de Janeiro gay and lesbian calendar. It takes place on Carnaval Tuesday and is packed with Rio celebrities. The event is televised both nationally and globally. 🅂 www.riogayguide.com/ carnival.htm

10 Publications and Websites
Brazil has no publications that cater solely to the gay and lesbian community. However, the website www.ipanema. com has a useful gay and lesbian directory section and a small amount of general information.

Left **Female dormitory of an Ipanema hostel** Right **A stall selling cheap tropical fruits**

🔟 Budget Tips

Book in Advance
Accommodations in Rio can be cheaper if you reserve in advance over the Internet. Many larger hotels offer as much as 30 percent off their rack rate for online bookings. It is normal to approach hotels in Rio directly and there is usually no need to go through a tour operator.

Travel Off-Season
Traveling to Brazil outside the popular tourist season can save as much as 50 percent on the cost of your trip. As well as this financial incentive, the beaches are far less crowded. The last two weeks of December through till Carnaval and June are busy, while April, May, August, and September tend to be much quieter.

Discount Plane Tickets
TAM, GOL, Webjet, and other Brazilian airlines offer cheap fights on the Internet. However, their websites only accept Brazilian credit cards, so book flights through your hotel if you can.
🕸 www.tam.com.br; www.voegol.com.br; www.webjet.com.br

Apartment Rental
If you are thinking of staying in Rio for more than a week, consider renting an apartment (see p115). These can be far cheaper than hotel rooms,

especially in the beach neighborhoods. Most come with a kitchenette and washing machine. They are an especially good deal for families.

Hostels
Most Rio hostels attract a young crowd, and offer private rooms as well as dormitory-style accommodations. These are usually – though not always – cheaper than most of the low-budget hotels. The most economical options are *com ventilador* (fan-cooled) only.

Cheap Eats
Prato feito set meals are an affordable lunch option, and are usually available in the cheaper Rio restaurants. Per-kilo restaurants are also reasonable, and are found all over the city (see p110). Many bars offer *petiscos*, or snacks, which are cheap and quick, and supermarkets and street vendors stock delicious and cheap tropical fruits.

Travel During Off-Peak Hours
Try to avoid taking taxis from 7am to 9am and from 4pm to 5pm, when Rio's traffic is very congested with commuters. If there is no metro to your destination, try to use it for at least part of your journey – you will save on time and money.

Laundrettes
Laundrettes, or *lavanderias*, in Rio are open from Monday to Saturday and are always at least 50 percent cheaper than the services offered by hotels. All laundrettes have attendants who can leave your wash load with and many will dry, fold, and even iron your clothes. Some will also deliver them to your hotel if the wash is pre-paid.

Sightseeing for Free
There's plenty to do in Rio for free. First and foremost is spending time on the city's many beaches. Aside from the Jardim Botânico (see pp18–19), all of Rio's parks are free, including Tijuca (see pp10–11), although there is often a cost in getting there. Most of Rio's churches do not have an admission charge. Many museums are free one day a week, usually Sunday.

Phone Cards
Newsstands and shops in the airports, bus station, and many Rio hostels sell discount *cartões telefonicos internacionais* (international phone cards). *Cartões telefonicas* (local phone cards) can also be bought at most newsstands, and are cheaper than using a cell phone, even with a Brazilian SIM card (see p105).

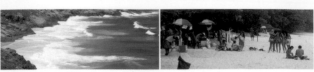

Left **Powerful waves hitting the shore** Right **Vacationers at the beach**

Top 10 Health and Security

1 Emergencies
The main emergency phone numbers in Rio de Janeiro city are as follows: Fire Department (Bombeiros) – 193; Police (Polícia) – 190; Ambulance (Ambulância) – 192. Although emergency numbers cater primarily to Portuguese speakers, the Tourist Police, on (021) 2332 2924, speak good English.

2 Pharmacies
Pharmacies, or *farmácias*, can be found throughout Rio, and hotels can usually advise on where to find those that offer a 24-hour service. Many prescription drugs, including antibiotics, are available over the counter in Brazil. As in Europe and North America, cosmetics, insect repellents, and sun protection can be purchased at pharmacies.

3 Travel Insurance
Visitors to Brazil should arrange travel insurance in advance. Robberies and snatch thefts are not uncommon and crimes should be reported immediately at a *delegacia* (police station). When reporting a crime, make sure to request an official printed report. Health insurance is necessary as ambulances take patients without insurance to public hospitals, where services and conditions may be poor.

4 Police
Rio's police force has only one English speaking office, specifically for tourists in Leblon – at the far southern end of Ipanema. At other police stations, generally only Portuguese is spoken.

5 Crime
Petty theft is common, especially on buses. Credit cards and other valuables are best stored in a zipped bag under your clothes or left at the hotel. Muggings are also not infrequent. It is best not to challenge the perpetrators. Avoid long walks after dark and use ATMs in malls and supermarkets rather than on the street.

6 Consulates
Foreign embassies are all in Brazil's capital, Brasília, but most countries have consulates in Rio. If you have a lost or damaged passport, contact your consulate. ✪ USA: http://riodejaneiro. usconsulate.gov/uscongen rj-info.html • Australia: www.dfat.gov.au/missions/ countries/brri.html • UK: www.reinounido.org.br

7 Beach Safety
During the day, Rio's beaches are generally well policed, but people should nonetheless bring as little as possible with them and stay alert. Personal items left on the beach are likely to be stolen, especially when it gets crowded.

8 Swimming Safety
There are strong currents and rip tides on many of Rio's beaches and the water is chilly. Look for lifeguard flags indicating unsafe areas for swimming. Swimming at some of the smaller, more obscure beaches is not advised as industrial outputs pour into the bay from Rio's northern suburbs and industrial operations. Stick to the beaches at Ipanema and beyond.

9 Discretion
Rio de Janeiro may appear liberal but it is actually quite conservative. Going topless is regarded as extremely vulgar on Rio beaches and could lead to arrest. *Samba* and *forró* involve very close dancing that is regarded as no more sexual than dancing apart to club music. Brazilians become offended when such dancing is confused with a proposition.

10 Drinking Water
Tap water in Rio is drinkable but not pleasant. Bottled water is plentiful and cheap but bring your own bottle as plastic waste is a huge problem. Many visitors buy a large bottle and use it to fill their own container. Most hotel lobbies and restaurants have a 5-gallon (20-liter) water dispenser with free chilled water.

Left **A beach at night** Center **One-way road sign** Right **A** *favela*

TOP10 Things to Avoid

1 Walking Around After Dark

Rio's city center is bustling and crowded during the day but surprisingly empty after 8pm. Be sure to take a taxi even for a journey of a few hundred yards. If you are stuck in an area with no apparent taxi stand, walk to the nearest hotel, bar, or restaurant and ask them to call a taxi. Cariocas are usually very obliging.

2 Beaches at Night

Rio's beaches are broad, long, and most are poorly lit at night. Thieves can approach quickly and leave rapidly, undetected. Stick to the well-lit streets that lie opposite the sand.

3 Dangerous Areas

Favelas should always be avoided except on organized tours with groups who contribute part of their income to the community. Never accept an invitation into a *favela* from someone you met on the beach. The city center, beaches, and quiet streets should be avoided after dark, as should Parque do Flamengo. Take care in and around the Rodoviaria Novo Rio, where thieves operate. ⊗ *Map H5, G6*

4 Unauthorised Taxi Cabs

Taxi cabs that cruise the streets looking for customers are generally safe but are occasionally used by unscrupulous or even unlicensed drivers. Take cabs from designated stands, hotels, or airport booths.

5 Insect Bites

In urban Rio, dangerous insects and arachnids are few and far between. However, mosquitoes are found in the city, and during particularly hot and wet periods, they commonly carry and transmit dengue fever – a viral infection with severe flu-like symptoms. Although there is no vaccine for it, visitors can protect themselves by using a good mosquito repellent (containing DEET) and choosing accommodation that is air-conditioned.

6 Sunburn

The tropical sun is strong. Use sunscreen of at least SPF 30. Children or those with sensitive skin should not use anything below SPF 50. Try to avoid being in direct sunlight between 11am and 1pm. Sunscreen is readily available in Brazilian pharmacies and supermarkets.

7 One-Way Road Systems

The beachfront streets in Ipanema, Leblon, and Copacabana are almost all one way. In an attempt to manage traffic, they change direction in the mornings and afternoons. On Sunday, some of the streets are closed altogether. As signage is very poor, heed the traffic or ask a local.

8 Prostitution

Prostitution is rife along Avenida Atlântica and in the various clubs and cafés that run along its length. Many transvestite prostitutes double up as muggers and the female prostitutes are famous for plying patrons with "Boa Noite Cinderelas" or "Good night Cinderellas" – drinks that have been drugged – and leave their clients with a hotel room empty of all their belongings.

9 Running Low on Change

Small shops and services rarely have change for notes larger than R$20. Be sure to keep a healthy wad of smaller notes in your pockets and keep the larger denominations stored under your clothing.

10 Speed Bumps

Speed bumps are called *lombadas,* or *quebra-moles,* and are common along the city's highways. They are twice the height and size of their European or US counterparts. The bumps are invariably signposted much earlier than they appear, either with their name or a silhouetted picture.

Left **A juice bar** Center **Tropical fruits** Right **Buffet at Arpoador Inn**

🔟 Dining Tips

1 Churrascarias
Brazilian spit-roast and barbecued meat restaurants are becoming popular the world over. Cuts of meat on skewers – from chicken hearts to loins of pork and fillet steaks – are brought to the table in a constant procession. Salads, beans, and rice are served at buffet counters. Rio has some of the best *churrascarias* in the country. On Sundays most serve the Brazilian national dish, *feijoada* – a thick meaty bean stew eaten with lime, manioc flour, and Brazilian raw cane rum, locally called *cachaça*.

2 Por-Kilo Restaurants
These buffet restaurants are among the best-value eating options in Rio and are especially popular at lunchtimes. Diners choose from a selection of self-serve dishes, which usually include some choices for vegetarians as well as a generous selection of very sweet desserts. The plates are then weighed and priced at the counter.

3 Meal Times
Cariocas usually eat breakfast between 7 and 9am. Lunch, which is the main meal of the day, is usually between noon and 2pm. Dinner tends to be light, except on special occasions, and is mostly eaten after 9pm.

4 Unrequested Appetizers
A number of restaurants place bread, olives, cold meats, and cheeses, known as *petiscos*, on the table. Although they appear to be free, these appetizers form part of a cover charge. To avoid paying, ask the waiter to take them away.

5 Set Lunch Menus
The *prato feito*, also known as P.F. or *prato de dia*, is a very cheap, and usually generous, lunchtime meal. It comprises a starter, a main course consisting of beef, chicken, or fish with french fries, beans, and rice, a dessert or juice, and coffee. Most smaller streetside restaurants offer this option, which is adver-tized with a P.F. sign.

6 Tipping
As in Europe, tipping in Brazil is always discretionary and should be given only for excellent service. Ten percent is considered a normal tip. Empty spaces near restaurants and bars are manned by unofficial parking attendants who "guide" your parking and offer to watch over your car. Cariocas usually pay them around R$5.

7 Vegetarian Restaurants
Vegetarians have a hard time in Brazil. When avail-able, choices tend to be limited to green salads with carrots and beetroot and fake meat dishes made with soya. Some of the better restaurants serve good vegetarian fare *(see pp44–5)*.

8 Hotel Restaurants
Some of Rio's best restaurants are found in hotels like the Copacabana Palace and the Fasano *(see p112)*. These are open to non-guests but should be booked ahead. Dress code at these restau-rants is generally more formal than in Rio's other dining establishments.

9 Padarias
Many bakeries in Rio double up as café-restaurants and often serve cheap *prato feito*. Snacks are also available and range from *misto quente* – melted cheese and ham with salad in a French bread roll – to energizing *açai na tigela* – ice-cold purple berries with *guaraná* syrup.

10 Fruit
Brazil has a delicious, cheap, and hugely varied choice of fruits, from familiar mangoes and papayas to the uniquely Brazilian, such as *açai*, a palm berry packed with vitamins and minerals, *cupuaçu*, a pungent white pod, and the delicate *umbu*. These can be bought in super-markets or as juice from juice bars.

Left **A room at a homestay** Center **Boutique hotel Casas Brancas** Right **A rental apartment**

TOP 10 Accommodation Tips

1 Choosing a Location

Security is an important consideration in Rio. The safer neighborhoods are Ipanema and Leblon, which are great for the beach, but are expensive and far from the city center. However, less secure neighborhoods, like Santa Teresa and the Guanabara Bay area, are culturally far richer.

2 Language Issues

Staff in the more expensive hotels and hostels often speak good English, but this is not the case in many of the cheaper establishments. It is a good idea to try to learn a few basic Brazilian–Portuguese phrases before your trip *(see pp126–7)*.

3 Reservations

The Brazilian high season is during Christmas and New Year as well as the two weeks around Carnaval when it is essential to book rooms well in advance. Reservations are also necessary for beach hotels on holiday weekends and must be made for the top luxury hotels at all times.

4 Discount Rates

Promotional discount rates are often available through hotel websites. These discounts can be up to 50 percent of the standard rate, especially if visitors reserve their room more than a few weeks in advance. It is always best to approach the hotel directly because discounts from their own sites are often better than those found on the international hotel websites.

5 Accommodation for Children

Extra beds, cots, and babysitting services are almost always available in Brazilian hotels. Most hotel restaurants will have special high-chairs for smaller children and a children's menu, which is usually cheaper than the adult menu.

6 Boutique Hotels

Stylish boutique hotels are fairly new to Brazil, which has generally preferred large, corporate towers. However, since the turn of the millennium, Rio has acquired quite a few of these charming establishments. They are mostly European-run and restricted to areas like Gávea, Santa Teresa, and the outer beaches beyond Ipanema.

7 Hostels

There are scores of hostels in Rio de Janeiro. Most are in the beach neighborhoods – notably Botafogo, Flamengo, Copacabana, and Ipanema. There is also a growing number in Santa Teresa. Websites like www.hostels.com and www.hostelbookers.com provide details of new and established hostels.

8 Homestays

Getting to know a Carioca is one of the best ways of getting to know the city. Socializing with one's host is up to guests – there is no pressure to do so and privacy is respected. Cama e Café offers homestays in Santa Teresa. Companies such as Angatu and The Brazilian Beach House Company offer private houses for rent.
$\searsow$ *www.camaecafe.com.br; www.angatu.com; www.brazilianbeachhouse.com*

9 Apartment Rental

Furnished apartments can be rented for stays of even a few days. The best have kitchens, washing machines, and satellite televisions, as well as concierge services and room cleaning every day. Prices range from US\$400 to US\$2,000 per month.
$\searrow$ *www.flatsinrio.com*

10 Concierges

Apartments, private homes, and most hotels have concierges. These can range from surly doorkeepers, or *porteiros*, to multilinguists who can recommend which dishes to eat in which restaurants. Being on friendly terms with the *porteiro* is important to Cariocas.

Ronnie Biggs's (see p82) flat is available for homestay with Cama e Café (see p115).

Left **Glória Palace** Center **Caesar Park** Right **Copacabana Palace**

10 Luxury Hotels

1 Fasano
Before this discreet, sophisticated five-star hotel opened in 2007, Ipanema and Leblon had no truly world-class luxury hotels. The rooms are beautifully appointed and have private balconies with sea views. The restaurant here is excellent. ◎ *Map P6 • Av Vieira Souto 80, Ipanema • (021) 3202 4000 • www.fasano. com.br• $$$$$*

2 Copacabana Palace
Copacabana's most plush hotel features ocean view suites that have housed princes, presidents, and visiting film stars. Portraits of many of the famous guests can be seen in the gallery. The older portion of the hotel has the best rooms. ◎ *Map R3 • Av Atlântica 1702, Copacabana • (021) 2548 7070 • www.copacabana palace.com.br • $$$$$*

3 Ipanema Plaza
This hotel occupies a tall tower a block from the sea at Ipanema's Arpoador end. The rooms on the "Ipanema floor" have clean modern lines and colors, along with Italian furniture. The top floor has a pool and offers great views of the Atlantic. ◎ *Map N6 • Rua Farme de Amoedo 34, Ipanema • (021) 3687 2000 • www.ipanemaplazahotel. com • $$$$$*

4 Caesar Park
Service is superb in Caesar Park, a business hotel overlooking Ipanema Beach. Views are excellent, as with the majority of Rio's tower-block hotels. There is 24-hour room service and beach facilities include sun-loungers and showers. ◎ *Map N6 • Av Vieira Souto 460, Ipanema • (021) 2525 2525 • www. caesarpark.com.br • $$$$$*

5 Sofitel
The fabulous views, excellent French restaurant Le Pré Catalan (see p91), and quality service are matched by the luxuriously appointed rooms. ◎ *Map Q5 • Av Atlântica 4240, Copacabana • (021) 2525 1232 • www. sofitel.com • $$$$$*

6 Glória Palace
Rio's grandest hotel in the 1920s is expected to reopen in 2014, completely refurbished but retaining much period charm. The hotel is particularly convenient for access to the city center, Lapa, and Aeroporto Santos Dumont. ◎ *Map X6 • Rua do Russel 632, Glória • (021) 2555 7272 • www. hotelgloriario.com.br • $$$$*

7 JW Marriott
This plush business hotel is one of Rio's finest in terms of service and business facilities, but the rooms are on the small side and many face inwards with views out over the atrium rather than the beach. ◎ *Map Q4 • Av Atlântica 2600, Copacabana • (021) 2545 6500 • www.marriott.com. br • $$$$$*

8 Sheraton Barra
These twin towers right on the beach are the best choice for stays in the outlying neighborhoods of Barra da Tijuca and Recreio dos Bandeirantes. The rooms are spacious and have balconies with sea views. ◎ *Map B6 • Av Lúcio Costa 3150, Barra da Tijuca • (021) 3139 8000 • www.shera ton-barra.com.br • $$$$$*

9 Pestana Rio Atlântica
The views out over Copacabana from this hotel's rooftop pool are some of the best in Rio. The rooms are well-decorated and all have balconies. ◎ *Map Q4 • Av Atlântica 2964, Copacabana • (021) 2548 6332 • www. pestana.com • $$$$$*

10 Royal Tulip São Conrado Beach
This former grand 1970s hotel between Leblon and São Conrado is undergoing a major refurbishment, which is due for completion in 2014. The adjacent beach is secluded and the views are stunning. ◎ *Map B6 • Rua Aquarela do Brasil 75, São Conrado • (021) 3323 2200 • www.inter*

Price Categories

For a standard, double room per night (with breakfast if included), taxes, and extra charges.

$	under US$50
$$	US$50–US$85
$$$	US$85–US$150
$$$$	US$150–US$200
$$$$$	over US$200

A Mama Ruisa suite

Boutique Hotels

1 La Suite
Rio's finest boutique hotel overlooks the exclusive Joatinga beach. Each of its seven rooms is painted a different color and has a lush marble bathroom to match. The overall theme is a blend of modern and classical styles. ◎ Map B6 • Rua Jackson de Figueiredo 501, Joatinga • (021) 2484 1962 • www. lasuiterio.com • $$$$$

2 La Maison
This sister boutique to La Suite is more understated and is a cab ride from the beach. It boasts fantastic views out to Corcovado. There are five rooms in assorted colors from hot pink to cool chinoiserie. ◎ Map D6 • Rua Sérgio Porto 58, Gávea • (021) 3205 3585 • www. lamaisonario.com • $$$$$

3 Marina All Suites
This plush seafront hotel, which has hosted countless celebrity guests, features eight signature suites created by leading designers. It also offers 30 additional suites with lounges and home theaters, and has a superb bar and restaurant. ◎ Map L6 • Av Delfim Moreira 696, Leblon • (021) 2172 1100 • www.marinaallsuites. com.br • $$$$$

4 Mama Ruisa
A charming, understated boutique hotel in a converted 18th-century mansion house in Santa Teresa. Each room is named after a different French cultural icon ◎ Map V6 • Rua Santa Cristina 132, Santa Teresa • (021) 2242 1281 • www. mamaruisa.com • $$$$$

5 Portinari Design
Copacabana's only boutique hotel has a series of designer suites in a business-like, tall, narrow tower. The decor is minimalist, the furnishings are functional, and the service attentive. ◎ Map Q5 • Rua Francisco Sá 17, Posto 6, Copacabana • (021) 3222 8800 • www. hotelportinari.com.br • $$$$

6 Casa 32
This mansion house has been lovingly restored and furnished. The atmosphere is intimate and the service attentive. There are only three suites, all of which overlook a little garden. ◎ Map Q3 • Largo do Boticário 32, Cosme Velho • (021) 2265 0943 • www. casa32.com • $$$$

7 Relais Solar
Decorated with hand-painted murals, Relais Solar has five spacious bedrooms, each with a private balcony and a view out over a lush garden to the city center. The huge windows keep the house bright and airy. ◎ Map V6 • Ladeira do Mereilles 32, Santa Teresa • (021) 2221 2117 • www. solardesanta.com.br • $$$

8 Arpoador Inn
Charmingly located right on the sand, this little tower block offers functional and basic rooms and facilities. The dining room opens onto the esplanade, allowing sunlight in during the mornings. ◎ Map P6 • Rua Francisco Otaviano 177, Ipanema • (021) 2274 6995 • www.arpoadorinn. com.br • $$$

9 Casa Áurea
This informal, family-run budget boutique hostel sits in its own little garden patio on a Santa Teresa backstreet. Each room is a different shape, size, and color, and is decorated with art. The crowd is young and the staff speak a variety of languages including English. ◎ Map V6 • Rua Áurea 80, Santa Teresa • (021) 2242 5830 • www. casaaurea.com.br • $$

10 Casa Mango Mango
Santa Teresa's most arty boutique hotel lies next to the convent that gave the neighborhood its name. The public areas and 10 rooms are decorated with works by local artists; there is also a dormitory with bunk beds. The rooms offer wonderful views over the tropical gardens to the city center. ◎ Map V6 • Rua Joaquim Murtinho 587, Santa Teresa • (021) 2508 6440 • www.casa-mangomango.com • $$

Recommend your favorite hotel on traveldk.com

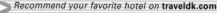

Left **Marina Palace suite** Center **Exterior of Sol Ipanema** Right **Mar Ipanema reception**

Mid-Priced Hotels

1 Marina Palace
One of the better tower hotels, the Marina Palace is within walking distance of Leblon's restaurants and has 109 spacious rooms. The upper floors have great ocean views. ✆ *Map L6 • Av Delfim Moreira 630, Leblon • (021) 2172 1010 • www.marinapalacehotel. com • $$$$*

2 Sol Ipanema
This beachside four-star hotel is the Ipanema representative of the Best Western chain. Rooms are a little small with standard hotel furnishings. The higher floors are quieter. ✆ *Map M6 • Av Viera Souto 320, Ipanema • (021) 2525 2020 • www.solipanema.com.br • $$$*

3 Copacabana Mar
This beachfront tower has comfortable rooms with minimalist, neutral decor and king-size beds. The hotel's business facilities are modern and include free access to wireless Internet in all rooms. ✆ *Map R3 • Rua Min. Viveiros de Castro 155, Copacabana • (021) 3501 7900 • www.copacabana mar.com.br • $$$*

4 Debret
Named for the French artist who painted some of the first landscapes of Rio, this modest, beachfront hotel has bright, airy rooms. Some suites have living areas with sofas, armchairs, and sturdy hardwood dining tables. ✆ *Map Q4 • Av Atlântica 3564, Copacabana • (021) 2522 0132 • www.debret. com • $$*

5 Ipanema Inn
There are good beach views from the upper floors of this tower, which is tucked behind the Caesar Park hotel in Ipanema. The hotel has plain but well-maintained rooms, and is close to the beach and shopping streets. ✆ *Map N6 • Rua Maria Quiteria 27, Ipanema • (021) 2523 6092 • www. ipanemainn.com.br • $$*

6 Mar Ipanema
This tower lies in the heart of Ipanema, near the beach and shopping areas. The simply decorated rooms have wooden floors and black and white prints of Rio. Use of beach chairs and towels is free. ✆ *Map M5 • Rua Visconde de Pirajá 539, Ipanema • (021) 3875 9191 • www.maripanema. com • $$*

7 San Marco
This two-star hotel is another simple but well-located tower hotel. Rooms are generally plain and minimally decorated but they vary so it is worth looking at a few before choosing. ✆ *Map M5 • Rua Visconde de Pirajá 524, Ipanema • (021) 2540 5032 • www. sanmarcohotel.net • $$$*

8 Hotel Vermont
The better rooms in this hotel are on the higher floors and have decent views, while the less desirable rooms on the lower floors overlook a concrete wall. This is one of the cheaper mid-priced options in the city and is very popular with the gay community. ✆ *Map N5 • Rua Visconde de Pirajá 254, Ipanema • (021) 3202 5500 • www.hotelvermont. com.br • $$$*

9 Savoy Othon Travel
The Savoy is part of the prosperous Brazilian Othon chain, but its rates are lower than many similar hotels in the area. Rooms on the upper floors boast fantastic views out over Copacabana. ✆ *Map Q4 • Av Nossa Senhora de Copacabana 995 • (021) 2125 0200 • www.othonhotels. com • $$*

10 Casa Cool Beans
This delightful B&B spread over four floors offers 10 luxurious, tastefully decorated rooms, plus gardens, a pool, and a sundeck. All rooms are en-suite and come with air conditioning, a mini bar, and free Wi-Fi access. A Brazilian-style breakfast is included. ✆ *Map U6 • Rua Laurinda Santos Lobo 146, Santa Teresa • (021) 2262 0552 • www. casacoolbeans.com • $$$*

Price Categories

For a standard, double room per night (with breakfast if included), taxes and extra charges.

$	under US$50
$$	US$50–US$85
$$$	US$85–US$150
$$$$	US$150–US$200
$$$$$	over US$200

The interior of a house on offer through Cama e Café

🔟 Apartments and Houses

1 Cama e Café
This homestay company has over 40 Santa Teresa houses on their books, from simple rooms in student houses to suites in Rio's most luxurious mansions. Guests can enjoy as much privacy or as much of the company of their host as they choose. ◎ Map U6 • Rua Paschoal Carlos Magno 90, Santa Teresa • (021) 2225 4366 • www.camaecafe.com • $$

2 Transamerica Prime Barra
These are spacious apartments, only a short walk from the beach, with Internet access, swimming pools, a restaurant, and room service. Close to Barra's shopping malls and nightlife, the apartments also feature views of the beach and Pedra da Gávea from the upper floors. ◎ Map B6 • Avenida Gastão Senges 395, Barra da Tijuca • (021) 2123 7000 • www.transamericaflats.com.br • $$$

3 Mercure Rio de Janeiro Arpoador
The apartments in this tall tower overlook Ipanema beach. The facilities and service here are similar to a hotel – there is room service, a business center, Internet access, parking, and a fitness center, pool, and a sauna. ◎ Map P6 • Rua Francisco Otaviano 61, Ipanema • (021) 2113 8600 • www.mercure.com • $$$$

4 Mercure Rio de Janeiro Ipanema
In a tower block between Copacabana and Ipanema, these apartments are a 5-minute walk away from both beaches. It has a pool, sauna, 55 well-appointed units that each come with separate living areas, and secure indoor car parking. ◎ Map P6 • Av Rainha Elizabeth 440, Ipanema • (021) 3222 9100 • www.mercure.com • $$$

5 Copacabana One Flat
These simple, small apartments come with a concierge service and sit six blocks from Ipanema and Copacabana beaches, near to Lagoa Rodrigo de Freitas. ◎ Map P4 • Rua Pompeu Loureiro 99, Copacabana • (021) 2255 3908 • $

6 Copacabana Holiday
These rental apartments are found in Copacabana, Ipanema, and Leblon, and many of them are located along the beachfront. Some are very good value. ◎ Map R3 • Rua Barata Ribeiro 90A, Copacabana • (021) 2542 1525 • www.copacabanaholiday.com.br • $$

7 Fantastic Rio
These studios and apartments, with up to five bedrooms as well as one- or two-floor penthouses, can be found throughout the city. It is one of the most established rental companies in Rio. ◎ (021) 3507 7491 • http://fantasticrio.br.tripod.com • $$–$$$$$

8 The Brazilian Beach House Company
This British-run company offers luxurious beach and town houses throughout Rio de Janeiro, as well as some beautiful properties in Búzios, Paraty, and Bahia. ◎ Rua Haddock Lobo 846, São Paulo (Headquarters) • (021) 2225 9476 • www.brazilian beachhouse.com • $$$$

9 Angatu
This company provides luxury private homes as well as private islands with cabins and yachts in the Paraty, Angra dos Reis, and Ilha Grande area. The service is excellent with full transfers available. ◎ www.angatu.com • $$$$

10 Rio Apartments
A range of comfortable apartments in Ipanema and Leblon, many of which have exclusive swimming pools, saunas, gym facilities, a concierge, room service, and chauffeur-driven car hire. ◎ Map N5 • Rua Rainha Elizabeth 85, Copacabana • (021) 2247 6221 • www.rioapartments.se • $$$

Left **Rio Hostel Santa Teresa** Center **Lemon Spirit Hostel** Right **Ipanema Beach House**

🔟 Budget Hotels and Hostels

1 Atlantis Copacabana

Although the air-conditioned rooms are small and simple, the location of this hotel could not be better – it is set in a quiet, safe area just a 2-minute walk from Copacabana and Ipanema beaches. Breakfasts are generous and there is a small rooftop pool.
🔇 *Map Q5 • Rua Bulhões de Carvalho 61, Copacabana • (021) 2521 1142 • www. atlantishotel.com.br • $$*

2 Stone of a Beach Hostel

One of Rio's top hostels for young backpackers sits near Copacabana Palace in one of the few old mansions in the Copacabana neighborhood. The adjoining Bar Clandestino shows cult and surf films when the dance floor is not pumping. 🔇 *Map R3 • Rua Barata Ribeiro 111, Copacabana • (021) 3209 0348 • www.stone ofabeach.com • $*

3 Ipanema Beach House

This is one of Rio's more upmarket hostels. Rooms and dorms are gathered around a pool and garden bar area with a kitchen and free Wi-Fi. The central Ipanema location is enviable and the beach is only a short walk away.
🔇 *Map M5 • Rua Barão da Torre 485, Ipanema • (021) 3202 2693 • www. ipanemahouse.com • $*

4 SESC Copacabana

This cultural center, built in a style made famous by the Brazilian architect Niemeyer *(see p68)*, features a theater, cinema, and hotel just one block from the beach. The atmosphere is quiet and the rooms are modern and well maintained. 🔇 *Map Q4 • Rua Domingues Ferreira 160, Copacabana • (021) 2548 1088 • www.sescrio. org.br • $*

5 Carioca Easy Hostel

Situated in Urca, one of Rio's safest neighborhoods, this hostel sits on a quiet backstreet near the waterfront. There are a handful of restaurants nearby and bikes are available to rent. 🔇 *Map J4 • Rua Marechal Cantuaria 168, Urca • (021) 2295 7805 • $*

6 Che Lagarto Hostel

This Argentinian, alligator-themed hostel chain is a popular party venue. Unlike most hostels, Che Lagarto does not offer a shuttle service. There is another branch in Copacabana. 🔇 *Map M5 • Rua Paul Redfern 48, Ipanema • (021) 2512 8076 • www.chelagarto.com • $*

7 Rio Hostel Santa Teresa

This hostel is built on the side of one of Santa Teresa's steep hills. It has its own pool and many of the rooms offer wonderful views of the city. 🔇 *Map V5 • Rua Joaquim Murtinho 361, Santa Teresa • (021) 3852 0827 • www.riohostel. com • $*

8 Sun Rio Hostel

The best small hostel in Botafogo, Sun Rio is situated in a converted town house close to Botafogo's restaurants and shops. Rooms are scrupulously clean. Some rooms have private bathrooms. 🔇 *Map H4 • Praia de Botafogo 462, Casa 5, Botafogo • (021) 2226 0461 • www. sunriohostel.com.br • $$*

9 Lemon Spirit Hostel

This small hostel, which has a tiny back patio and a little bar, is one of the very few cheap options in Leblon. It lies in a converted town house with four- and six-bed dormitories. 🔇 *Map L5 • Rua Cupertino Durão 56, Leblon • (021) 2294 1853 • www.lemonspirit.com • $*

10 Casa 6

This French-owned hostel on a side street has a number of poorly ventilated rooms, so make a point of checking out a few before you settle in. The hostel is quiet and does not attract the regular party crowd. 🔇 *Map M5 • Rua Barão da Torre 175, Casa 6, Ipanema • (021) 2247 1384 • www. casa6ipanema.com • $*

Price Categories

For a standard, double room per night (with breakfast if included), taxes, and extra charges.

$	under US$50
$$	US$50–US$85
$$$	US$85–US$150
$$$$	US$150–US$200
$$$$$	over US$200

Beautiful views from Abracadabra's swimming pool

TOP 10 Hotels in Rio State

1 Casas Brancas
Búzios's plushest hotel comprises a series of mock-Moorish villas on the side of a hill overlooking the Atlantic and the Ilha Branca. The town center and the best of the restaurants and shops are a 5-minute walk away and beach buggies are available for hire. The hotel has an excellent spa, an infinity pool, and three atmospheric restaurants. ⌖ Map C2 • Alto do Humaitá 8, Búzios • (022) 2623 1458 • www.casasbrancas.com.br • $$$$$

2 Abracadabra
This establishment offers the same enviable views out over the Atlantic as its sister hotel, Casas Brancas, but the rooms are smaller and plainer and the rates are cheaper. ⌖ Map C2 • Alto do Humaita 13, Búzios • (022) 2623 1217 • www.abracadabra pousada.com.br • $$$$

3 Pousada da Alcobaça
This enchanting pousada near Petrópolis offers 11 tastefully furnished rooms in an early 20th-century house, set amid magnificent grounds complete with a pool, tennis court, and nature trail. Gourmet meals are available. ⌖ Map B2 • Rua Agostino Goulao 298, Correas, Petrópolis • (024) 2221 1240 • www.pousadada alcobaca.com.br • $$$$

4 Sagu Mini-Resort
At this romantic island hideaway, nine rooms with balconies and surrounded by tropical gardens overlook the bay. Facilities include a restaurant and a solar-heated springwater hot tub. ⌖ Map A2 • Praia Brava, Abraão, Ilha Grande • (024) 3361 5660 • www.saguresort.com • $$$$$

5 Hotel Donati
Itatiaia's best hotel is set in the midst of the rain forest, and has a pool and restaurant. Trails lead from the cabins into the national park and with enough notice, the hotel can organize guides. ⌖ Map A2 • Estrada do Parque Nacional Km 9.5, Parque Nacional Itatiaia • (024) 3352 1110 • www.hoteldonati.com.br • $$$

6 Hotel Chalés Terra Nova
With charming cabanas on the edge of the rain forest, this hotel features a pool in a peacock- and hummingbird-filled tropical garden. The hotel also organizes light adventure activities. ⌖ Map A2 • Estrada do Parque Nacional Km 4.5, Parque Nacional do Itatiaia • (024) 3352 1458 • www.chalesterranova.com.br • $$

7 Solar do Império
The most luxurious hotel in Petrópolis is housed in a classically furnished 19th-century mansion on the city's grandest avenue, within walking distance of the principal sights. The hotel facilities include an excellent restaurant. ⌖ Map B2 • Av Koeler 376, Petrópolis • (024) 2103 3000 • www.solar doimperio.com.br • $$$$

8 Pousada do Sandi
The most comfortable and well-appointed of all the pousadas in Paraty's colonial center has a spa, a good restaurant, and a bar. ⌖ Map A2 • Rua do Rosário 1, Paraty • (024) 3371 2100 • www.pousada dosandi.com.br • $$

9 Pousada Literária de Paraty
This hotel offers 11 luxuriously fitted rooms facing onto an outdoor pool. The two suites on the upper floor are among the best rooms in town. ⌖ Map A2 • Rua do Comércio 362, Paraty • (024) 3371 8325 • www.hotelcoxixo.com.br • $

10 Bromelias Pousada and Spa
Featuring luxury cabanas set in the heart of the Mata Atlântica rain forest, this hotel spa offers a range of treatments from reiki to aromatherapy massage. The hotel has a pool, tennis courts, and a decent restaurant. ⌖ Map A2 • Rodovia Rio-Santos (BR–101) Km 558, Graúna, Paraty • (021) 3371 2791 • www.pousada bromelias.com.br • $$$$

A pousada is a guesthouse, often housed in an historic building.

General Index

00 (Zero Zero) 47
66 Bistro 77

A

Abracadabra 117
Academia da Cachaça 46
accommodations
  apartment rentals 107,
    111, 115
  boutique hotels 111, 113
  budget hotels 116
  homestays 111
  hostels 107, 111, 116
  hotels in Rio State 117
  luxury hotels 112
  mid-priced hotels 114
  reservations 107, 111
  tips 111
Adega do Pimenta 85
Adega do Timão 62
Aeroporto Internacional
  Antônio Carlos Jobim
  103
Aeroporto Santos Dumont
  53, 103
airports 103
Albamar 63
Alberto, Carlos 43
Alcaparra 71
Alda Maria 85
Alessandro e Frederico 91
Al-Kuwait 63
Amarelinho 62
Andrea Saletto 90
Angatu 115
Anima Mundi – Festival
  Internacional de Cinema
  de Animação 33
Antiquarius 44
Antônio Bernardo 55
apartment rentals 107, 111,
  115
Aprazível 85
Arabe da Gávea 77
Arcos da Lapa 82

Armazém 16,184
Arpoador beach 37, 51
Arpoadar Inn 113
Atlantis Copacabana 116
ATMs 105

B

Bacalhau do Rei 77
Baile do Copa 40
baile funk 39
Baile Vermelho e Preto do
  Flamengo 41
Baixo Bebê 27, 48
Baixo Gávea 73
Banda de Carmen Miranda
  41
Banda de Ipanema 40, 106
banks 105
Bar Brasil 62
Bar do Arnaúdo 85
Bar do Mineiro 85
Bar Jóia 76
Bar Lagoa 76
Bar Luíz 47, 62
Bardot 47
Baronneti 46
Barra da Guaratiba 51
Barra da Tijuca 36
Barracuda 71
bars and nightclubs 46–7
  Lagoa, Gávea, and
    Jardim Botânico 76
  Santa Teresa and Lapa
    84
Bartholomeu 99
beaches
  Arpoador 37, 51
  Barra da Guaratiba 51
  Barra da Tijuca 36
  Botafogo 37
  Charitas 36
  Copacabana 7, **24-5**,
    36, 87

beaches (cont.)
  Flamengo 37
  Grumari 36, 51
  Ipanema 7, **26–7**, 36,
    53, 87
  Itacoatiara 51
  Itaipu 51
  Leblon 7, **26–7**, 36, 51, 87
  Fora 68
  Prainha 51
  Recreio dos
    Bandeirantes 37, 51
  São Conrado 36, 51
  Vermelha 68
beach exercise 27
beach massage 27
beach safety 108, 109
beach soccer 25, 43
beach vendors 25
beach volleyball 27, 50
beachwear 26
Beco das Sardinhas 62
Belmonte IV 76
Ben, Jorge 33
Biggs, Ronnie 82
bird-watching 18, 98
Bistro do Paço 63
Bistrô dos Correios 63
Bloco Cacique de Ramos
  40
Bloco de Segunda 40
Bloco Santa Teresa 40
boat tours 53
Bon Vivant Bistrô e
  Delicatessen 71
bossa nova 33, 38, 88
Botafogo beach 37
botecos 60 see also bars
  and nightclubs
boutique hotels 111,
  113
Le Boy Carnaval Ball 106
Braseiro da Gávea 77
Brasserie Europa 63

The Brazilian Beach House Company 115
Bromelias Pousada and Spa 98, 117
Buarque, Chico 33
budget hotels 116
Burle Marx, Roberto 70, 73
buses 103
Búzios 95

C

cable car 12
Cabo Frio 51, 97, 98
Caesar Park 112
Café Botânico 19
Café do Lage 77
Café do Theatro 63
Café Lamas 71
Cais do Oriente 63
Cama e Café 115
Candelária Church 60
car rental 103
Carioca da Gema 46, 83, 84
Carioca Easy Hostel 116
Carlos Tufvesson 90
Carlos, Roberto 33
Carmen Miranda 41 *see also* Museu Carmen Miranda
Carnaval 32, 35, 40–41
Caroline Café 76
Casa 6 116
Casa 32 113
Casa Aurea 113
Casa Cool Beans 114
Casa da Feijoada 91
Casa da Mãe Joana 83, 84
Casa da Suiça 71
Casa de Arte e Cultura Julieta de Serpa 70
Casa de Cultura Laura Alvim 88
Casa de Rui Barbosa 69
Casa Mango Mango 113

Casa Turuna 55
Casas Brancas 117
Cascatinha do Taunay 10
Castelinho do Flamengo 70
Catedral Metropolitana de São Sebastião 60
Catimbaú 97, 99
Celeiro 91
cell phones 105
Centro 58–63
    botecos and cafés 62
    restaurants 63
Chácara do Céu 81
Chafariz da Glória 70
Chafariz do Mestre Valentim 23
Champions' Parade 40
Charitas beach 36
Che Lagarto Hostel 116
children
    accommodation 111
    activities 48–9
    play areas 27
    travel 104
choro 38
Christ the Redeemer *see* Cristo Redentor
churches
    Candelária Church 60
    Catedral Metropolitana de São Sebastião 60
    Igreja Nossa Senhora da Glória do Outeiro 67
    Igreja de Nossa Senhora do Monte do Carmo 23, 59
    Igreja da Ordem Terceira de Nossa Senhora do Carma da Antiga Sé 23, 59
    Igreja Santa Cruz dos Militares 22
    Igreja Santo Antônio 60
    Mayrink Chapel 11

churches (cont.)
    Mosteiro de São Bento 6, **14–15**, 59
    Nossa Senhora da Lapa 61
churrascarias 110
Cidade Negra 33
Cigalon 99
Cipriani 91
Circo Voador 83-4
climate 102
Clube dos Democráticos 83-4
Confeitaria Colombo 61-2
consulates 102, 108
Convento de Santa Teresa 82
Copacabana Mar 114
Copacabana Palace 24, 40, 87, 112
Copacabana *see* Praia de Copacabana
Copacabana, Ipanema, and Leblon 86–91
    places to eat 91
    shopping 90
Corcovado 6, **8-9**, 53, 75
credit cards 105
crime 108
Cristo Redentor 8–9, 10–11, 67, 75
cruises 53, 98
Cunhambebe 31
currency 105
customs and duty 102
cycling 26

D

Da Fonseca, Marechal Deodoro, 31
Da Silva, Leônidas 43
da Vila, Martinho 33
Dama da Noite 84

Debret 114
de Sá, Mem 31
de Sá, Sandra 33
Dia do Índio 32
Didi 43
disabled travelers 104
diving 51, 98
do Amaral, Tarsila 17
Dom Pedro I, Emperor 20, 30, 31
Dom Pedro II, Emperor 11, 20, 21, 30, 31, 67, 95
driving 103, 109
driving tours 53, 98

E

electricity 104
embassies 102, 108
emergency 108
Escadaria Selarón 82
Espaço Cultural da Marinha 48
Espírito Santa 45, 83, 84
Esplanada Grill 45
Estação das Barca 23
Estádio do Maracanã 12, 35, 42, 52

F

Fasano 45, 112
favelas 52, 74
Feira de São Cristóvão 54
Feira do Rio Antigo 83
Feira Hippie Market 54, 90
Fellini 91
ferries 97, 103
Festa de Nossa Senhora da Penha 32
Festa de São Sebastião 32
Festa Literária Internacional de Paraty (FLIP) 33, 97
Festas Juninas 33
festivals and shows 32-3 see also Carnaval
Festival Internacional de Cinema de Rio 33

fishing 97
Flamengo beach 37
Floresta da Tijuca 9, 53
footvolley 27, 43
Fora beach 68
Forneria São Sebastião 91
Fortaleza de São João 70
Forte de Copacabana 25
Forte Duque de Caxias 25

G

gafieira 38
Gala Gay 41, 106
Garcia and Rodrigues 54
Garcia d'Ávila, Ipanema 87, 89
Garota da Gávea 76
Garota de Ipanema 88
Garrincha 43
Gávea see Lagoa, Gávea, and Jardim Botânico
Gay Pride Parade 106
gay travelers 106
Gero 45
Gérson 43
Getúlio 55
Gilson Martins 90
Le Gite D'Indaiatiba 99
Glória Hotel 112
golf 51
Goya Beira 85
Grumari beach 36, 51
The Guanabara Bay Beach Neighborhoods 66-71
boat tours 53
places to eat 71
Guimas 77

H

hang gliding 11, 50
health 102, 108
helicopter tours 9, 12, 49, 53
hiking 50, 52
Hipódromo Up 76
history of Rio de Janeiro 30-31

homestays 111
Horto Florestal 74
hostels 107, 111, 116
hotel booking 107, 111
Hotel Chalés Terra Nova 117
Hotel Donati 117
Hotel Vermont 114
hotels see accommodations

I

Igreja Nossa Senhora da Glória do Outeiro 67
Igreja de Nossa Senhora do Carmo da Antiga Sé 23, 59
Igreja da Ordem Terceira de Nossa Senhora do Monte do Carmo 23, 59
Igreja Santa Cruz dos Militares 22
Igreja Santo Antônio 60
Ilha Fiscal 35
Ilha Grande 53, 97
Instituto Moreira Salles 73
inter-city buses 103
Internet cafés 105
Ipanema 7, **26–7**, 36, 53, 87 see also Copacabana, Ipanema, and Leblon
Ipanema Beach House 116
Ipanema Inn 114
Ipanema Plaza 112
Itacoatiara beach 51
Itaipu beach 51

J

Jairzinho 43
Jardim Botânico 7, **18–19**, 48, 73, 75 see also Lagoa, Gávea, and Jardim Botânico

Jardim Zoológico 48
Joâo VI, King 7, 18, 20, 22–3, 30–31
Jobim, Antônio Carlos 27, 88
Jorge, Seu 33
Jota Bar 76
JW Marriott 112

K

King Joâo VI see Joâo VI, King
kite surfing 50
Kubitschek, Juscelino 31

L

Lagoa, Gávea, and Jardim Botânico 72-7
  night spots 76
  restaurants 77
language 102, 105, 111
Lapa see Santa Teresa and Lapa
Largo das Neves 81
Largo do Boticário 74
Largo dos Guimarães 81
laundrettes 107
Leblon 7, 26–7, 36, 51, 87
  see also Copacabana, Ipanema, and Leblon
Leme 24
Lemon Spirit Hostel 116
Lenny 54
Les Artistes 77
lesbian travelers 106
live acts and shows 33
Livraria da Travessa 55
Locanda della Mimosa 99
luxury hotels 112

M

La Maison 113
Mama Ruisa 113
Manekineko 45
Mar Ipanema 114

Maracanã Stadium see Estádio do Maracanã
Margutta Citta 63
Maria Bonita 90
Marina All Suites 113
Marina da Glória 70
Marina Palace 114
Mata Atlântica 95, 96, 98
Mayrink Chapel 11
Melt 47
Memorial Getúlio Vargas 70
Mercure Rio de Janeiro Arpoador 115
Mercure Rio de Janeiro Ipanema 115
Merlin O Mago 99
metrô 103
Miam Miam 71
mid-priced hotels 114
Mike's Haus 85
Mirante Andaime Pequeno 11
Mirante Dona Marta 11
Mistura Fina 46
mobile phones 105
money 105
Monte, Marisa 33
Monumento Nacional dos Mortos de II Guerra Mundial 67
de Moraes, Vinícius 27, 88
Morro da Urca 12, 69
Morro do Leme 25, 89
Mosteiro 63
Mosteiro de São Bento 6, **14–15**, 59
Mr Lam 77
Museu Carmen Miranda 67
Museu Casa Benjamin Constant 53, 82
Museu Casa dos Pilões 19
Museu da República 34
Museu de Arte Contemporanea do Niterói (MAC) 34

Museu de Arte Moderna (MAM) 35
Museu de Folclore Edison Carneiro 68
Museu do Carnaval 35
Museu do Indio 68
Museu H. Stern 89
Museu Histórico Nacional 7, **20–21**, 34, 59
Museu Imperial, Petrópolis 95
Museu Internacional de Arte Naïf (MIAN) 34
Museu Nacional 35
Museu Nacional de Belas Artes 6, **16–17**, 34, 59, 61
Museu Villa-Lobos 68
museums 34–5
music 38, 55

N

New Natural 91
New Year's Eve, Copacabana 25, 32
newspapers 104
Niemeyer, Oscar 31, 35, 68
nightclubs see bars and nightclubs
Niterói 36, 53
Nossa Senhora da Lapa 61
Nuth 47

O

O Boticário 54
O Paladino 62
off-season travel 107
Olympe 44
opening hours 104
Orquestra Imperial 33
Orquidarium 19
Os Dois Irmãos 27, 48, 53, 87
Os Esquilos 10

outdoor activities 50–51
  beach exercise 27
  beach massage 27
  beach soccer 25, 43
  beach volleyball 27, 50
  bird-watching 18, 98
  boat tours 53
  cruises 53, 98
  cycling 26
  diving 51, 98
  driving tours 53, 98
  fishing 97
  footvolley 27, 43
  golf 51
  hang gliding 11, 50
  helicopter tours 9, 12, 49, 53
  hiking 50, 52
  kite surfing 50
  paragliding 50
  rock climbing 13, 51
  running 26, 50
  soccer 42-3
  surfing 50
  trails, treks, and walks 10, 13, 98, 109
  wildlife spotting 11, 13, 98
  windsurfing 50

P
Paço Imperial 22, 61
padarias 110
pagode 38
Pagodinho, Zeca 33
Palácio Gustavo Capanema 70
Palácio Tiradentes 23
Palaphita Kitsch 76
Pão de Açúar see Sugar Loaf Mountain
Paraty 53, 97, 98
paragliding 50
parks and green spaces
  Horto Florestal 74

parks and green spaces (cont.)
  Jardim Botânico 7, 18–19, 72, 73
  Jardim Zoológico 48
  Parque da Catacumba 49, 73, 75
  Parque do Cantagalo 75
  Parque do Flamengo 70
  Parque Lage 53, 75
Parque da Catacumba 49, 73, 75
Parque do Cantagalo 75
Parque do Flamengo 70
Parque Lage 53, 75
Parque Nacional da Tijuca 6, 10–11, 52
Parque Nacional do Itatiaia 49, 96, 98
Pedra da Gávea 11, 53
Pestana Rio Atlântica 112
petiscos 110
Petrópolis 53, 95, 98
pharmacies 108
phone cards 107
Pista Cláudio Coutinho 13, 69
Planetário 49, 74
police 108
Porcão Rio's 71
Porta Kent Pizzeria 85
Portinari Design 113
post offices 105
Pousada da Alcobaça 117
Pousada Literária de Paraty 117
Pousada do Sandi 117
Praça XV 7, 22–3, 59, 61
Praia de Copacabana 7, 24–5, 36, 87
Prainha beach 51
prato feito (P.F.) 107, 110
Le Pré Catalan 91
Presente de Yemanjá 32
Prince Regent João see João VI, King
private drivers 103

prostituition 109
public holidays 104
public telephones 105
Punta Di Vino 99

Q
Quadrífoglio 77

R
Raajmahal 71
Raiz Forte Produtos da Terra 90
rap brasileiro 39
Real Gabinete Português de Leitura 60
Recreio dos Bandeirantes 37, 51
Região dos Lagos 96
Regua 98
Relais Solar 113
repente 39
reservations 107, 111
restaurants 44
  Centro 62–3
  cheap eats 107
  churrascarias 110
  Copacabana, Ipanema, and Leblon 91
  dining tips 110
  The Guanabara Bay Beach Neighborhoods 71
  Lagoa, Gávea, and Jardim Botânico 77
  prato feito (P.F.) 107, 110
  Rio de Janeiro State 99
  Santa Teresa and Lapa 85
Rio de Janeiro State 95-9
  accommodations 117
  activities 98
  places to eat 99
Rio Hiking 52, 69, 75
Rio Hostel Santa Teresa 116
Rio Minho 62
Rio Scenarium 46, 83, 84

Rio Water Planet 49
Roberta Sudbrack 44
Rocinha *favela* 27, 53, 74
rock climbing 13, 51
Romário 43
Ronaldo 43
Royal Tulip São Conrado
    Beach 112
Rua Dias Ferreira 88, 89

S
Sacrilégio 84
Sagu Mini-Resort 117
samba 33, 38
samba funk 38
samba schools 41
samba soul 39
Sambódromo 35, 40
San Marco 114
Sansushi 85
Santa Teresa and Lapa
    80-85
    bars and clubs 84
    places to eat 85
Santos, Nilton 43
São Conrado beach 36, 51
Saturnino 76
Satyricon 44, 99
Savoy Othon Travel 114
Scala 41, 106
security 108, 109
Serra dos Órgãos 95, 98
SESC Copacabana 116
SESC Cultural Centers
    104
Sheraton Barra 112
shopping 54
    Copacabana, Ipanema,
    and Leblon 90
Shopping Rio Design 90
Sobrenatural 85
soccer 42-3
Sofitel 112
Sol Ipanema 114
Solar do Império 117
Stone of a Beach Hostel
    116

Sugar Loaf Mountain 6,
    12-13, 48, 53, 67, 69
suinge 38
La Suite 113
Sun Rio Hostel 116
surf beaches 51
surfing 50
Sushi Leblon 91

T
tap water 108
taxis 103, 109
Teatro Municipal 16, 61,
    63
Teatro Odisséia 84
telephones 105
Tempo Glauber 70
Teresópolis 96
Thai Paraty 99
theft 108
tipping 110
tips 111
Toca do Vinícius 55, 90
Toulon 90
tour operators 102
tourist information 104
tram rides 81
Transamerica Flat Barra 115
transport 103
    air 103
    buses 103
    car rental 103
    driving 103, 109
    inter-city buses 103
    metrô 103
    private drivers 103
    taxis 103, 109
    tram rides 81
travel insurance 108
traveler's checks 105
Travessa do Comércio 23,
    61, 62
treks, trails, and walks 10,
    13, 98, 109

Trem do Corcovado 9
Trem do Corcovado
    Museum 9

V
vaccines 102
vanguarda 39
Vargas, Getúlio 31
Vermelha beach 70
Victor Hugo 90
Villa Verde 99
visas 102

W
War Memorial, Glória *see*
    Monumento Nacional
    dos Mortos de II Guerra
    Mundial
War of the Triple Alliance
    17, 21, 25
weather 102
websites 104
wildlife spotting 11, 13, 98
windsurfing 50
women travelers 104

Y
Yorubá 71

Z
Zazá Bistrô Tropical 91
Zico 43
Zuka 44

Acknowledgments

The Author
Alex Robinson is a writer and photographer based in the UK and Brazil. He has worked for DK, *New York Times, Departures, Sunday Times Travel, M, Marie Claire,* and *Nota Bene* among other publications and specializes in luxury travel, adventure, and Lusitanian culture and music. Find out more about him on www.alexrobinsonphotography.co.uk

Publisher
Douglas Amrine

List Manager
Christine Stroyan

Managing Art Editor
Mabel Chan

Senior Editor
Sadie Smith

Project Editor
Alexandra Farrell

Project Designer
Shahid Mahmood

Senior Cartographic Editor
Casper Morris

Senior Cartographer
Suresh Kumar

Cartographer
Jasneet Kaur Arora

DTP Operator
Natasha Lu

Production Controller
Imogen Boase

Photographer
Alex Robinson

Additional Photography
Demetrio Carrasco

Fact Checkers
Huw Hennessy, Suzana Wester dos Santos Ribeiro

Revisions Team
Louise Abbott/cobalt id; Shruti Bahl, Marta Bescos; Louise Cleghorn; Emer FitzGerald; Maite Lantaron; Jude Ledger; Carly Madden; Rada Radojicic; Ellen Root

Picture Credits
a = above; b = below/bottom; c = center; l = left; r = right; t = top.

Works of art have been reproduced with the kind permission of the following copyright holders:

www.tarsiladoamaral.com.br *Auto–retrato* ou *Le Manteau Rouge* 16cl; Candido Portinari (1903–1962) *Café,* oil on canvas, 1935, Reproduction authorized by Joao Candido Portinari 16bc.

The photographer, writers, and publisher would like to thank the media staff at the following sights and organizations for their helpful cooperation:

4CORNERSIMAGES: SIME/Hans Peter Huber 4–5.

Courtesy of www. ABRACADABRA.COM.BR: 117tl. AGENCIA O GLOBO: Marcelo Carnaval 32tc; Monica Imbuzeiro 15bc, 32tr; Andre Teixeira 40tr; Marco Antonio Teixeira 49tr. ALAMY: Brazil Photos/Ricardo Beliel 52b; Laura Coelho 18c; Chad Ehlers 64–5; Iconotec 32b; Wolfgang Kaehler 13bl; Mountain Light/Galen Rowell 10–11c; South America 78–9; The London Art Archive 30bl; travel44 3tr, 38b; Peter Treanor 25cra, 32tl; Andrew Woodley 41tl. ANTONIO BERNARDO: 55tr.

Courtesy of BEST WESTER SOL IPANEMA HOTEL: 114tc. THE

BRIDGEMAN ART LIBRARY: *Independence or Death, the Shout of Ipiranga on the 7th September 1822* (oil on canvas), Don Pedro di Figueredo Americo (1843–1905) 30t. Courtesy of BURLE MARX & Cia.LTDA: 73b.

Courtesy of CASAS BRANCAS BOUTIQUE–HOTEL & SPA: 111tc. COLEÇÃO MUSEU NACIONAL DE BELAS ARTES/IPHAN/MinC.: photo Vicente de Mello 16cl; photo Jaime Acioli 17cr; detail photo César Barreto 17cb. CORBIS: JAI/ Jane Sweeney 3bl; Joao Luiz Bulcao 43tl; Gregg Newton 103tl; David Pollack 9tr; Jose Fuste Raga 56–7.

FSB COMUNICACOES: Marluce Balbino 12cb; Robson Santos 6cr.

GETTY IMAGES: Gallo Images/ Roger de la Harpe 25–26c.

Courtesy of HOTEL FASANO, RIO DE JANEIRO: 44bl. Courtesy of HOTEL MARINA PALACE: 114tl.

Courtesy of LEMON SPIRIT HOSTEL: 116tc.

Courtesy of www.MAMARUISA. COM: 113tl. MUSEU HISTÓRICO NACIONAL: 7ca, 20cb, 20–21c, 21bl; Ricardo Bhering 21t.

PHOTOLIBRARY: Japan Travel Bureau 26–7c; Photononstop 92–3; Robert Harding Travel 28–9. Courtesy of www.POSTO9.`COM: 40tl.

Courtesy of RIO HOSTEL, IPANEMA: 107tl. Courtesy of RIO HOSTEL, SANTA TERESA: 116tl. Courtesy of www.RIOAPART MENTS.COM: 111tr. Courtesy of www.RIOGAYPARADE.COM: 106tl. Courtesy of www. RIOHIKING.COM.BR: 13cra.

TYBA AGENCIA FOTOGRAFICA: J.R.Couto 70tl; Rogerio Reis 39tl; M.A.Rezende 70tr.

VISAGE MEDIA SERVICES: Time & Life Pictures 31tl.

All other images are © Dorling Kindersley. For further information see *www.dkimages.com.*

Special Editions of DK Travel Guides

DK Travel Guides can be purchased in bulk quantities at discounted prices for use in promotions or as premiums. We are also able to offer special editions and personalized jackets, corporate imprints, and excerpts from all of our books, tailored specifically to meet your own needs.

To find out more, please contact:
(in the United States) **SpecialSales@ dk.com**
(in the UK) **travelspecialsales@uk.dk. com**
(in Canada) DK Special Sales at **general@tourmaline.ca**
(in Australia) **business.development@ pearson.com.au**

Phrase Book

In an Emergency

Help!	**Socorro!**	sookorroo
Stop!	**Pare!**	pahree
Call a doctor!	**Chame um médico!**	shamih oong mehjikoo
Call an ambulance!	**Chame uma ambulância!**	shamih ooma amboolans-ya
Where is the hospital?	**Onde é o hospital?**	ohnd-yeh oo oshpital
Police!	**Polícia!**	poolees-ya
Fire!	**Fogo!**	fohgoo
I've been robbed	**Fui assaltado**	fwee asaltadoo

Communication Essentials

Yes	**Sim**	seeng
No	**Não**	nowng
Hello	**Olá**	ohla
How are you?	**Como vai?**	kohmoo vī
Goodbye	**Tchau**	tshow
See you later	**Até logo**	ateh logoo
Excuse me	**Com licença**	kong lisaynsa
I'm sorry	**Desculpe**	dishkoolp
Thank you	**Obrigado** *(if a man is speaking)*/	obrigadoo/
	obrigada *(if a woman is speaking)*	obrigada
Good morning	**Bom dia**	bong jeea
Good afternoon	**Boa tarde**	boh-a tarj
Good evening/ night	**Boa noite**	boh-a noh-itsh
Pleased to meet you	**Muito prazer**	mweengtoo prazayr
I'm fine	**Estou bem/ tudo bem**	shtoh bayng/ toodoo bayng
What?	**O que?**	oo kay
When?	**Quando?**	kwandoo
How?	**Como?**	kohmoo
Why?	**Por que?**	poorkay

Useful Phrases

On the left/right	**À esquerda/ direita**	a-shkayrda/ jirayta
I don't understand	**Não entendo**	nowng ayntayndoo
Please speak slowly	**Fale devagar por favor**	falee jivagar poor favohr
What's your name?	**Qual é o seu nome?**	kwal eh say-oo nohm
My name is…	**Meu nome é…**	may-oo nohm eh
Go away!	**Vá embora!**	va aymbora
That's fine	**Está bem**	shtah bayng
Where is…?	**Onde está/ fica…?**	ohnj shtah/feeka
Is this the way to the…?	**Este é o caminho para…?**	aysht-yeh oo kameen-yoo pra

Useful Words

big	**grande**	granj
small	**pequeno**	pikaynoo
hot	**quente**	kayntsh
cold	**frio**	free-oo
bad	**mau**	mow
good	**bom**	bong
open	**aberto**	abehrtoo
closed	**fechado**	fishadoo
dangerous	**perigoso**	pirigohzoo

safe	**seguro**	sigooroo
first floor	**primeiro andar**	primayroo andar
ground floor	**térreo**	tehrryoo
lift	**elevador**	elevadohr
toilet	**banheiro**	ban-yayroo
men's	**dos homens**	dooz ohmaynsh
women's	**das mulheres**	dash mool-yehrish
late	**tarde**	tarj
now	**agora**	agora
entrance	**entrada**	ayntrada
exit	**saída**	sa-eeda
passport	**passaporte**	pasaportsh

Post Offices & Banks

bank	**banco**	bankoo
bureau de change	**(casa de) câmbio**	(kaza jih) kamb-yoo
exchange rate	**taxa de câmbio**	tasha jih kamb-yoo
post office	**correio**	koorray-oo
postcard	**cartão postal**	kartowng pooshtal
postbox	**caixa de correio**	kīsha jih koorray-oo
ATM	**caixa automática**	kīsha owtoomatshika
stamp	**selo**	sayloo
cash	**dinheiro**	jeen-yayroo
withdraw money	**tirar dinheiro**	tshirar jeen-yayroo

Shopping

How much is it?	**Quanto é?**	kwantweh
I would like…	**Eu quero…**	ay-oo kehroo
clothes	**roupa**	rohpa
This one	**Esta**	ehshta
That one	**Essa**	ehsa
market	**mercado**	merkadoo
Do you accept credit cards?	**Aceitam cartão de crédito?**	asaytowng kartowng jih krehditoo
expensive	**caro**	karoo

Sightseeing

museum	**museu**	moozay-oo
art gallery	**galeria de arte**	galiree-a jih artsh
national park	**parque nacional**	parkee nas-yoonal
beach	**praia**	prī-a
river	**rio**	ree-oo
church	**igreja**	igray-Ja
cathedral	**catedral**	katidrow
district	**bairro**	bīrroo
garden	**jardim**	Jardeeng
tourist office	**informações turísticas**	infoormasoyngsh ooreeshtsheekash
guide	**guia**	gee-a
guided tour	**excursão com guia**	shkoorsowng kong gee-a
ticket	**bilhete/ ingresso**	bil-yaytsh/ ingrehsoo

Transport

bus	**ônibus**	ohniboosh
boat	**barco**	barkoo
train	**trem**	trayng
airport	**aeroporto**	a-ayroopohrtoo
airplane	**avião**	av-yowng
flight	**vôo**	voh-oo